Contents

Trademarks

All terms mentioned in this book that are known to be trademarks or service marks are listed below. In addition, terms suspected of being trademarks or service marks have been appropriately capitalized. Alpha Books cannot attest to the accuracy of this information. Use of a term in this book should not be regarded as affecting the validity of any trademark or service mark.

America Online is a registered trademark of America Online, Inc.

CompuServe is a registered trademark of CompuServe Incorporated, an H&R Block company.

GEnie is a registered trademark of General Electric.

Windows is a trademark of Microsoft Corporation.

MS-DOS, MS, and Microsoft are registered trademarks of Microsoft Corporation.

Introduction

So you've found your way to the Internet. You've heard how you can send e-mail across the world, how you can copy files from computers the other side of the globe back to your computer, how you can search databases on any conceivable subject, how you can meet people with your interests. But now that you're connected, it all looks a little daunting. Just how do you *do* all this?

Now that you're on the Internet, you've discovered it's not quite so straightforward. Do you use Gopher or Veronica, the World Wide Web or a Wide Area Information Server? And what's all this about FTP and Telnet? Do you need them? And if so, how do you use them?

You don't really care about all this stuff, anyway. You just want to get to the goodies on the Internet, with minimal hassle. You don't want to become a computer genius. You just want to experience the wonders of the Information Highway.

What Is the Internet?

Unlike the many commercial online information sources available—CompuServe, America Online, GEnie, and so on—the Internet is a collection of networks, a giant agreement among thousands of computer systems to connect together. The Internet contains

- Government computers, owned by nations throughout the world.

- Computers run by hundreds of different universities and schools.

- Systems owned by large corporations, such as IBM and Microsoft.

- Systems belonging to non-profit organizations that just want to bring online computing "to the people."

- Computers owned by commercial enterprises that make money by providing people with access to this amazing interconnected system.

The Internet connects millions of people throughout the world, from Russia to Rhode Island, Austria to Australia. Once on this fantastic system—if you know where you are going and how to get there—you can cruise around in cyberspace, traveling from computer to computer, continent to continent.

Even though there are many goodies to be gathered, there's a catch—the Internet can be difficult to use, even downright confusing. It isn't owned by a single commercial organization that needs to please customers in order to survive, so the Internet's "user interface" is, in general, clunky and outdated. If you like working at a UNIX or DOS prompt, you'll feel right at home on the Internet. But if you're used to the world of the "graphical user interface"— Windows, OS/2, the Mac, and so on—you'll find the Internet primitive and confusing.

You need the *10 Minute Guide to the Internet*.

What Is the 10 Minute Guide, and Why Do You Need It?

You need help to find your way around. The *10 Minute Guide to the Internet* uses a series of lessons to help you find your way around the Internet quickly and with no fuss. Each lesson is designed to take ten minutes or so and teach you the basic skills you need to get around.

But Every System Is Different...

There's another problem with the Internet. Because it's a collection of thousands of different systems hooked together, there are many different ways to work on the Internet. There *are* nice graphical user interfaces for the Internet, though most users don't have access to them. For instance, there's a free program called Mosaic that runs on the Macintosh and with Windows. It's a neat system that makes some aspects of the Internet easy to use—but most people are not working on systems that are running Mosaic. So the *10 Minute Guide to the Internet* was written with the majority of Internet users in mind. We are going to assume that our readers...

- Have some kind of simple "terminal" connection to the Internet. Perhaps you are using a terminal connected to your university's or company's system that is connected to the Internet (and the company hasn't installed one of these fancy new user interfaces). Or maybe you are dialing into a local "service provider's" computer using some kind of simple data communications program, such as Windows Terminal, Qmodem, CrossTalk, or whatever.

- Are connected to a UNIX "host." Most of the Internet's host computers run an operating system called UNIX. There are a few running other operating systems, but the majority of Internet users connect through UNIX machines, so we are going to use UNIX examples.

Conventions Used in This Book

You'll find procedures explained in simple English in this book. With straightforward, easy-to-follow steps—and special icons to call your attention to important tips and definitions—this book can make learning about the Internet quick, clear, and easy. The following icons help you find your way around:

Plain English Definitions clarify new terms.

Timesaver Tips offer hints for using the
Internet more effectively.

Panic Button icons identify places where new
users can run into trouble.

To make your Internet cruising more efficient, you'll
find a table of UNIX commands and a glossary of Internet
terms at the end of the book. Throughout the *10 Minute
Guide to the Internet*, specific conventions help you find
your way around the Internet as easily as possible:

Menu names	The names of menus, commands, buttons, and dialog boxes are shown with the first letter capitalized for easy recognition.
Numbered steps	Step-by-step instructions are given bold color numbers, so you can find basic Internet procedures easily.
What you type	Within the numbered steps, color text shows you the keys you press and the information you type.
placeholders	These italicized words show you where to supply your own specific information.
what you see on the screen	A special font indicates examples of what appears on-screen.

The *10 Minute Guide to the Internet* gets you started in twenty lessons. These range from basic logging in to more advanced Internet activities. Most new users will want to start at the beginning, and master the lessons one at a time.

For Further Reference...

The *10 Minute Guide to the Internet* teaches you enough to find your way around the Internet. It may be all you need. But if you decide you'd like a bit more detail, I suggest that you check out *The Complete Idiot's Guide to the Internet*, by Peter Kent.

Lesson

How Will You Connect?

In this lesson you learn about the different types of Internet connection.

The Four Types of Internet Connections

There are four basic types of Internet connection, all of which have to be connected to an Internet *host*. A host computer is connected directly to the Internet, and has an Internet address—other computers on the Internet can send messages to this computer.

Permanent Connections

Many users have computers or terminals that are wired directly to one particular computer, which is in turn permanently connected to the Internet. This is the best type of connection, but unless your university or employer has provided you with a system, you won't have one—it costs tens of thousands of dollars to set up. This sort of connection is often known as a *permanent direct* or *dedicated* connection.

Dial-in Direct Connections

Some *service providers*—organizations that provide access to the Internet—let you dial into their computer across a phone line, and then switch into *dial-in direct mode*. Your computer acts as if it were a host on the Internet—for instance, files that you copy from other computers are sent directly to your computer, not to the service provider's computer. This is the second-best type of connection, but it can be expensive and complicated to set up. This sort of connection is often known as a *SLIP*, *CSLIP*, or *PPP* connection.

Dial-in Terminal Connections

Many service providers have *dial-in terminal* accounts. You dial across the phone lines, but your computer stays in a "terminal" mode once it connects to the service provider's computer. It doesn't appear to be connected to the Internet directly; it's just a terminal connected to the service provider's host computer. For instance, when you copy files from a computer on another continent, they are copied back to your service provider's host computer. You then have to transfer them back to your own computer, using your communications program's data transfer commands. These are often known as *dial-up* or *interactive* connections.

Mail Connections

Some Internet users have only mail access to the Internet. They can send and receive mail, but that's it. It's possible to use many of the Internet's special features "through the mail," but it's like trying to tie your shoes wearing boxing gloves—you can do it, but it'll take plenty of practice—so we're not going to discuss it in this book.

What Type Do You Have?

I'm going to assume that you have either a permanent connection or a dial-in terminal connection. The mail connections are very limited in capabilities, and the dial-in direct connections are a completely different way of working with the Internet.

Once you have a dial-in direct account, you can pick and choose from a variety of different user interfaces for various different procedures on the Internet. (You could install one of those fancy Macintosh or Windows interfaces, for example, if you have the time and skills necessary to install them.) But there's a problem with such accounts—they are more expensive, and more complicated.

Most Internet users are working with either a permanent or dial-in terminal connection. It's pretty easy to figure out the type you have. If all you can do is send and receive mail, you've got a mail connection (and this book won't help you). If you connect to a service provider by dialing in across the phone lines using a non-Internet-specific communications program—the sort of program with which you could dial *any* computer information service—you have a dial-in terminal account. And if you don't have to dial into the Internet at all, just get on through your university's or employer's computer by selecting an option from a menu or running a command, you have a permanent connection.

What About the User Interface?

The term *user interface* refers to the tools a computer provides for you to communicate with the computer and tell it what you want to do. A *GUI* (graphical *user interface*) gives you graphics (visual images) as tools to work with. For instance, to carry out a command with Windows or a Macintosh, you put the mouse pointer on a small square on the screen (a *button* or *icon*) and click. You may also be able to select commands from *drop-down menus*. GUIs make using a program relatively easy, because you don't have to remember too much—everything's right there in front of you.

With a *command-line* interface, you have to type commands. Basic DOS and UNIX use command-line interfaces. Whereas in a GUI you might be able to drag a picture of a computer file to a picture of a "trash can" icon to delete the file, in a command-line interface you type a command and name the file you want to delete.

It's true that command-line interfaces are quick (if you know the program well), but they have fallen out of favor because they make it hard to learn a new program and remember how to use it. Unfortunately, most Internet users are forced to use the command line on occasion, though usually they also have access to simple, non-graphical menus or lists of options from which they can select.

The GUI is the mode of the future for the Internet. For now, though, the user interface most Internet users are working with is the simple menu and the command line. And that's the user interface I assume you have.

In this lesson you learned about the various types of Internet connections. In the next lesson, you learn about the equipment you need to connect to the Internet.

Lesson

Picking Your Equipment

2

In this lesson you learn about the equipment and information you'll need before you can connect to the Internet.

Which System Do You Have?

In the first lesson, you learned about the types of Internet connection. As I explained in that lesson, I'm going to assume that you have either a permanent connection (a terminal computer connected to an Internet host computer owned by a government department, university, school, or business), or a dial-in terminal connection. If you have a dial-in direct connection—a PPP or SLIP connection, for instance—you're in the wrong book!

> **Host Computer** A *host* computer is one that is directly connected to the Internet, generally providing service to a number of people using computer terminals or actual computers connected to the host computer.

If you are using a permanent connection to the Internet, preparing to get onto the Internet is usually a simple matter—you use the equipment provided to you by your system administrator.

System Administrator   The term *system administrator* means the person in charge of maintaining the host computer, whether he's an employee of your university or company, or someone at the service provider's office.

The computer that your terminal or computer is connected to is already connected to the Internet (your system administrator will handle the details of how it's all hooked together), so you don't have to do anything special to get started. Like the dial-in account users, though, you still need a login name and password (more about these later in the lesson).

If you have a dial-in account, you need to call the host computer and make a connection. You need more equipment than the permanent-connection user does.

What Equipment Do You Need?

Here's what you need to make the connection:

- An Internet account
- A computer
- A modem
- Simple communications software
- Communications parameter information
- A login name
- A password

An Internet Account

I'm assuming you have already chosen a service provider, and signed up for an Internet account. If not, you might want to check out *The Complete Idiot's Guide to the Internet* (Peter Kent, Alpha Books), which contains detailed information on picking a service provider or FreeNet, and even has discount coupons from several service providers.

A Computer

You don't need a fancy computer to access the Internet. If your computer can run telecommunications software and be connected to a modem, you can use it on the Internet, whether it's an old Mac or PC, or the most up-to-date workstation, PowerPC, or Pentium machine.

A Modem

The *modem* converts your computer's digital signals to analog signals that can be transmitted on the phone lines. You really need a fast modem, preferably 9,600 *bps* (bits per second) or even 14,400 bps. You might get by with 2,400 bps, but anything slower will probably be unbearable.

If you already have a modem, try using that. If you plan to buy one, ask the system administrator for the features that will work best with his or her system. You can get high-quality 14,400-bps modems for around $130 to $170.

Simple Communications Software

You don't need fancy communications software to get onto the Internet—but of course, if you spend much time online, you'll appreciate the useful tools provided by the better programs. You do have to have a program that can do *xmodem* data transfers (most can), or better still, *zmodem* transfers (many can). And you need a program with *VT100 or VT102 terminal emulation* (most have this).

> **VT100 and VT102** The VT100 and VT102 terminals are Digital Equipment Corporation products that have become a standard for computer terminals. Many communications programs can *emulate*—imitate—these terminals.

> With terminal emulation, when your computer connects
> to the host computer, what you see on the screen looks
> much the same as it would if you were working on a real
> VT100 or VT102 terminal.

You may already have a telecommunications program.
Most modems these days come with a program such as
Qmodem or CrossTalk. Many *integrated* packages (such as
Microsoft Works) come with telecommunications programs.
And if you have Microsoft Windows, you have Windows
Terminal. We'll be using Terminal for the examples in this
book.

Communications Parameters

If you are going to dial into the Internet host, you need to
know how to set up your communications software. Your
system administrator should be able to provide certain
information to you—you need to know the *data bits*, *stop
bits*, *parity*, and *flow control* settings. It doesn't really matter
what these terms mean—they're just different ways in which
computers can transmit information to each other, and they
have to be set correctly or your communications session
won't work. Also, ask your system administrator what type
of terminal emulation you should use. In most cases VT100
or VT102 mode works fine.

A Login Name

Your system administrator must give you a *login name*.
This is simply a name the computer you will connect to
can recognize you by. For instance, John Smith might
have *Jsmith* or *johnS* as his login. This login name is *case-
sensitive*. That is, the characters must be typed in the
correct uppercase or lowercase format—John Smith
won't be able to type *JSMITH* or *jsmith* if his login name
is actually *Jsmith*, for instance.

Other Terms   You will also hear the terms *logon name, username,* and *account name.* They all mean the same thing.

A Password

Not only do you have to identify yourself to the Internet host you connect to, but you also have to confirm that you are who you say you are. You do this by typing a *password,* a special word that (in theory) nobody else knows. Usually this can be up to eight characters long, and you will be issued one when you first get your Internet account (you may tell the system administrator what you want to use, or that person may simply pick one for you).

The first time you log into the Internet, you should change your password—so that if anyone else has seen it between the time the system administrator issued it and you received it, they won't be able to use it. Like the login name, the password is also case-sensitive.

Here are a few tips for picking a password:

- Don't pick a password that someone might guess. Here are some examples that are *too easy*: a child's name, your car's number plate, or a character from *The Lord of the Rings.*

- The best password is a random jumble of characters: *1n=9YT%*, for instance.

- Random jumbles are difficult to remember, so create what appears to be a random jumble—mix special characters with several short words—for example, *I&you%in.* You could pick three short words at random from a dictionary.

- Don't give your password to anyone else—and if you do, change it as soon as he or she is finished.

- Don't type your password while someone is watching—and if you do, change it as soon as he or she leaves.

- Change the password regularly—every month, for instance. (Some systems may force you to do so, stopping you from logging in until you create a new password.)

- Don't write the password online anywhere (in messages, for instance).

- The longer the password, the better. Five characters is too short. Ask your service provider the maximum password length (probably eight characters).

I Forgot!   If you forget your password, don't worry. Call the service provider. Someone there can assign you a new one. Use it to log in, then change it again.

In this lesson you learned about the equipment and information you will need before you can connect to the Internet. In the next lesson, you learn how to set everything up before dialing into the host computer.

Lesson

3

Getting Ready to Dial

In this lesson you learn how to prepare your computer for connecting to the Internet. If you are working with a permanent connection, skip to Lesson 5.

Installing Your Modem and Software

The first step is to install your modem and software, if you haven't done so already. Modems come in two types, *external* and *internal*. The electronics are much the same, but one connects to your computer's serial port outside the computer, and the other is installed inside the computer. Installing a modem is usually fairly straightforward, but make sure you read all the installation instructions carefully.

Preparing the Software

Next you must tell the software how you want it to act. Each software package is different, of course, but they have many similarities. As an example I'm going to use Windows Terminal—the telecommunications program that comes Microsoft Windows, Windows for Workgroups, and Windows NT. Millions of people have this simple program; we can use it to demonstrate the basic procedures you'll carry out (whatever program you use). If you are using another program, yours may work a little differently, so check your documentation.

Start the Program

Start your communications program. In the case of Windows Terminal, you can start it by simply double-clicking on the Terminal icon in the Accessories program group, or by selecting the icon and pressing Enter.

Entering the Phone Number

The first step is to enter the phone number you wish to dial. Follow these steps:

1. Open the Settings menu and select Phone Number. The Phone Number dialog box appears.

2. Type the telephone number given to you by your service provider into the Dial text box. Don't forget to include any numbers you must dial for an outside or long-distance line.

Figure 3.1 The Phone Number dialog box.

3. Click on the OK button to close the dialog box.

There are several optional settings you can adjust in the Phone Number dialog box. They are:

Timeout If Not Connected In This means the amount of time you want to wait after dialing the call—if your modem hasn't connected to the service provider's modem within that time, it will stop trying. Leave this as it is for now; you may want to come back and change it later.

Redial After Timing Out   This option tells the program to try dialing the call again if it was unable to connect within the time you specified—if, for instance, the line was busy. If you want to use this option, click on the check box.

Signal When Connected   This option tells the program to sound the computer's beep when connected. If you want to use this option, click on the check box.

When entering the phone number to dial, keep in mind that you may need to dial additional numbers first, such as a 1 for long distance or a 9 for an outside line. (Normally when you dial 9 for an outside line, you pause a moment to wait for your phone system to connect. You can include a one-second pause in Terminal with a comma. Figure 3.1 shows a number with a two-second pause after dialing the 9.)

Hold My Calls   If the line you are using has call waiting, you will want to turn off that feature before calling the Internet; enter the code (usually *71) that turns it off. (Call waiting tones can disturb your Internet session, even causing you to lose data.)

Selecting a Terminal Type

Once your computer is connected to the service provider's computer, it's going to act as a *terminal*, a brainless viewscreen that simply displays what it is told to display. Since Terminal is capable of imitating several types of terminal, you must tell Terminal which type the service provider's computer expects. Here's how.

1. Open the Settings menu and select Terminal Emulation to see the dialog box in Figure 3.2.

Figure 3.2   The Terminal Emulation dialog box.

2. Unless your service provider has told you otherwise, select VT100. Other programs have more options, but again, select VT100 (or VT102), unless told otherwise.

3. Click on OK to close the dialog box.

Terminal Setup

The next step is to tell Terminal how to behave while it is "emulating" (imitating) a terminal. Follow these steps:

1. Open the Settings menu and select Terminal Preferences to see Figure 3.3.

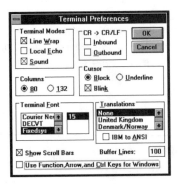

Figure 3.3   The Terminal Preferences dialog box.

2. Make changes as desired to the settings.

3. Click on OK when you're finished.

Here are brief descriptions of the options you can choose from, and some advice for choosing their settings:

Line Wrap   Leave Line Wrap selected. This tells Terminal to wrap long lines onto two lines if necessary, rather than just throw away the text at the end of the line.

Local Echo   Leave Local Echo unselected, unless you run into problems later. Most systems are *full duplex*: when you type a character, it's sent by the modem to the other computer, which instantly "echoes" it back—so it appears on your computer screen. If you are connecting to a computer that is "half duplex" (unlikely), you will want to use Local Echo so Terminal itself displays the text you type, without waiting for it to be sent back from the other computer.

Sound   The Sound option is not important—it lets the other system get to your computer's beeper, which few systems will try to do anyway.

CR->CR/LF   You can usually leave the CR->CR/LF options turned off. These tell Terminal to add a *linefeed* (that is, move to the next line) each time it gets a *carriage return* instruction from the other computer (that is, an instruction to move back to the left column). Most computers do this automatically.

Columns   You can set up the number of text Columns you want—you'll probably want to use 80, though if you have a large screen you might use 132.

Cursor   Select one of the Cursor types, and whether it should Blink. These options simply define what the cursor will look like on your screen during a session.

Terminal Font   Terminal Font simply defines what
the characters in the window will look like while you
are working. You can experiment with different fonts,
but for now you'll probably want to leave it alone.

Translations   Translations are used if your computer
is using a character set different from the one used by
the service provider's computer—again, you'll generally leave this alone.

Show Scroll Bars   This option turns scroll bars on
and off for the Terminal window. If you have scroll
bars turned on, you can scroll back to see text that has
scrolled off the top of the screen.

Buffer Lines   This setting specifies the number of
lines that you can scroll if you use the scroll bars to
see text that has scrolled off the top of the screen.
(Once you've exceeded the number of buffer lines,
the oldest lines are lost as new ones arrive.)

**Use Function, Arrow, and Ctrl Keys for
Windows**   Clear this check box. If it's selected, you
won't be able to use the Arrow and Ctrl keys, which
your service provider's computer will expect you to
be able to do. (Some Windows communications
programs will automatically turn off these keys—so if
you want to select text from the screen during a
session, for instance, you have to use the menu commands, not the Windows Ctrl+C command.)

Communications Parameters

Now let's tell the program how it will communicate with the
host computer's modem.

1. Select the Communications option from the Settings
   menu to see Figure 3.4.

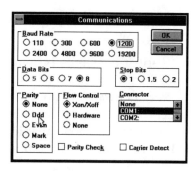

Figure 3.4 The Communications dialog box.

2. In the Baud Rate area, select the maximum speed that your modem and the service provider's modem can both support. (*Baud rate* is much the same as bps—bits per second—though purists would say that modem speed is actually bps.) If the box doesn't include your modem's speed (14400, for instance), select the next highest (19200).

3. Click on the correct Data Bits option button. This— and the information for steps 4 through 6—should be given to you by your system administrator.

4. Click on the correct Stop Bits option button.

5. Select the correct type of Flow Control.

6. Select the correct type of Parity.

7. Select the communications port you are using from the Connector list, it's usually COM1 or COM2. If you aren't sure, experiment—Terminal may tell you if you've chosen wrong, and when you come to dial (next lesson), you'll soon know if you got the right one.

8. Click on OK when you're finished.

You can also alter these less-common settings in the Communications dialog box:

Parity Check   Parity Check tells Terminal to display a question mark when it receives a character that it knows has an error (a character with a "parity error"). If you don't select this option, it simply displays a garbage character, even if it knows that it's wrong. You don't need to worry about this option now.

Carrier Detect   You probably won't need Carrier Detect—try it if your modem is unable to connect to the service provider's computer (assuming you are sure that everything else is set correctly).

Modem Setup

Now tell the program how to communicate with your computer's own modem. Follow these steps:

1. Open the Settings menu and select Modem Commands to see the dialog box in Figure 3.5.

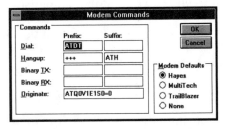

Figure 3.5   The Modem Commands dialog box.

2. Select one of the Modem Defaults from the box on the right. Select Hayes compatible if you're not sure which type you have.

3. If your telephone line is a "pulse" line, change the Dial entry to ATDP. You can generally leave the rest of this box's options alone.

Save Your Setup

Now you need to save your settings. Open the File menu and select Save. You'll be asked to provide a filename—type INTERNET and click on OK. The next time you want to log into the Internet you can open this file (using the Open command on the File menu), so you won't have to enter the data each time.

Fancy Software Features

If you have a more sophisticated communications program than Terminal, you may have some extra toys you can play with. You may be able to create your own toolbar buttons, for instance, and program them to carry out certain actions when you click on them (similar to Terminal's Function keys, but perhaps more advanced). Or you may be able to get your program to "record" a login script, so it will log in automatically for you each time.

> **Login Script**   A login script is simply a procedure that a communications program uses to automate the connection, entering your login name and password for you.

Read your software manual to find out what you can do. Right now you may not see how the features can help you, but as you play with the Internet, you'll find procedures that you may want to automate.

In this lesson you learned how to prepare your system before connecting to the Internet. In the next lesson, you learn how to dial into the host computer.

Lesson

Going Online

In this lesson you learn how to dial into your service provider's host computer and log into the Internet. If you are working on a permanent connection, skip to Lesson 5.

Before Going Online

Before you go online, you might want to consider what you're going to do when you get there. In most cases it will be obvious once you've logged in—the information on the screen will tell you what to do (or what you can do). In other cases, you may have various options that you have to know about before logging on. For instance, you may be able to type **menu** to see a menu of options, or **shell** to see the UNIX command line. Ask your service provider about the procedure for logging in, or read the documentation you were given.

Dialing Into the Host Computer

Now you're going to take a look at a sample session. Your procedure may be a little different, but the principles are the same. I'm using Windows Terminal again—your communications program may work a little differently.

1. Open the Phone menu and select the Dial option. Your modem starts dialing, as you can see in Figure 4.1. The first lines you see at the top of the window are simply your computer communicating with your modem.

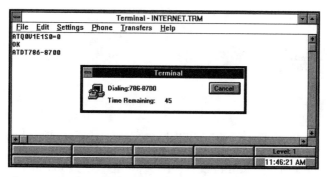

Figure 4.1   Dialing the host computer.

2. If the system you are calling is not busy, within a few seconds your modem will connect to the modem at the other end (see Figure 4.2). You'll see some information identifying the system you are connecting to, and then you'll be asked for your login name (in this case, your *username*, but remember, they're the same thing.)

> **Extra Typing Required**   Before asking for your login name, some systems may ask for some other kind of information—for instance, The Pipeline, a service provider in New York, asks you to type the word *pipeline* before logging on. Your service provider will tell you what you need to type, if anything.

Figure 4.2   The login prompt.

3. Type your login and press Enter. (Remember to type the login *exactly* as it was given to you, capitalizing letters where necessary.) You'll be asked for your password.

4. Type your password and press Enter. Again, make sure you type it exactly as it was given to you, capitalizing letters where necessary. Type carefully, because you won't see what you type—the other computer won't "echo" the typing back to your system, so anyone looking over your shoulder can't see what your password is.

> **Login Incorrect!** You may see a message saying *Login incorrect*. This means that either the name or password was wrong. Try again, being very careful to type exactly the login name and password you were given. Try a few times, if necessary—but if you still can't get into the system, you may have an incorrect login name or password. Call the system administrator to check.

5. Once your login has been approved, you're into the system.

What Next?

Now that you're into the system, what do you do? That depends on the system you're working with. Each is a little different. Figure 4.3 shows what you'd see if you logged into the Colorado SuperNet system, a service provider in Golden, CO.

Figure 4.4 shows you what you'd see if you logged into the Pipeline, a service provider in New York.

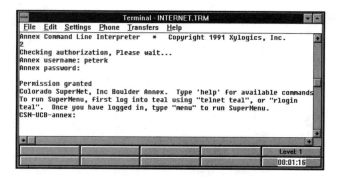

Figure 4.3 The Colorado SuperNet screen.

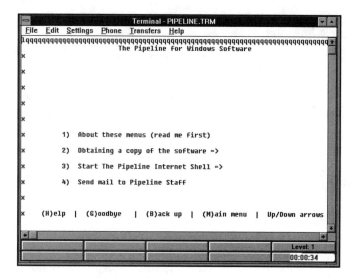

Figure 4.4 The Pipeline screen.

In most cases, you can simply follow onscreen instructions, or at least written instructions that have been given to you. In the case of the Colorado Supernet, I type rlogin teal, then type menu. (*Teal* is the name of the host computer.) I then see a screen like the one in Figure 4.5.

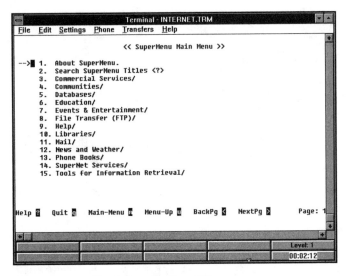

Figure 4.5   The Colorado SuperNet menu.

When working with the Pipeline, I have to select the Start the Pipeline Internet Shell option; the screen in Figure 4.6 appears.

> **Windows Interface?**   The Pipeline is one of the few service providers that has a Windows interface for its dial-in terminal users. I'm not going to describe this interface, as most people won't be using such a program. But the Internet is moving in this direction; someday soon, most of us will be working with neat graphical user interfaces. For now, back to reality.

The Command Line

There's something else you might see now, something a lot less "friendly." Many users may be faced with a *command line*, a UNIX prompt that is waiting for you to type a command. Figure 4.7 shows such a command line.

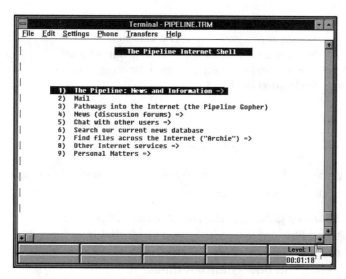

Figure 4.6 The Pipeline Internet Shell menu.

Figure 4.7 The UNIX command line.

Your command may look different. The name will usually be different (in Figure 4.7, *teal* is the name of the host computer my system is connected to), and the character after the host name may not be % (you may see a $ instead).

Operating System   UNIX is an *operating system*, a program that tells a computer's hardware what each application program wants it to do, and vice versa. Many host computers on the Internet use UNIX.

Running into Problems

You may find yourself with any one of a variety of problems while dialing into the Internet.

You see garbage on the screen.   If you see something like __p/÷__#£ä__, you've probably got something set incorrectly. Check your baud rate, stop bit, parity, and flow control settings.

You see something like ~~xx~xxx~xx.   Your baud rate may be set incorrectly.

You see something like this at the beginning of lines: ^7M or ^K or ;H2J;H2J24. You may be using the wrong terminal type.

Your service provider has a menu system you should be seeing, but all you see is a jumbled mess.   You're probably using the wrong terminal emulation.

You can't see the characters you type.   Turn Local Echo on.

You see every character you type twice.   Turn Local Echo off.

There's a blank line after each line of incoming text.   Turn Inbound CR/LF off.

There's a blank line after each line of outgoing text. Turn Outbound CR/LF off.

Incoming text is displayed on one line. Turn Inbound CR/LF on.

Backspace Won't Work? If you can't get your Backspace key to delete the preceding character while working online, try the Delete key, Ctrl+h, or #.

Not Your Fault Not all problems are at your end—your service provider can also screw up and enter your account information incorrectly. If you are still having problems after you've checked everything at your end, call your service provider and describe the symptoms. In particular, make sure you are using the correct login name, password, and terminal type.

In this lesson you learned how to dial into the Internet. In the next lesson, you learn how to get around a menu system (if available), how to change your password, and how to log off.

Lesson

Working Online

*In this lesson you learn how to work online, how to
change your password, and how to log off the system.*

Where Are You?

In the last lesson I described how to dial into the Internet
and log on. Now I'm going to assume that, whether you
have a permanent connection or a dial-in terminal connection, you are logged into the Internet.

You may see a menu of some kind, or you may see a
UNIX command line, something like *teal%* or *teal$*. (The
word—*teal* in this case—is the name of the host computer.
The character—% or *$*—simply tells you the system is
waiting for you to type a command.) The figures in the
previous lesson show examples of a couple of different
menus and a command line.

Using the Menus

If you are lucky, you have some kind of menu system to
use. The one shown in Figure 5.1 is from Colorado
SuperNet. It's worth taking a look at, because it's a *gopher*
menu system. You learn more about gophers in Lesson 12,
but for now let's just say that gophers provide a relatively
easy way to get around the Internet, and sometimes are
used as a service provider's primary interface.

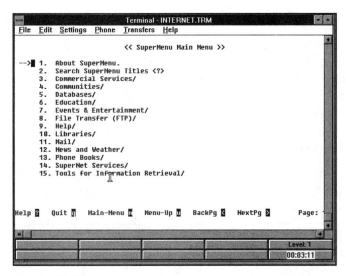

Figure 5.1 A typical menu system, based on a gopher.

The menu you see will help you find your way around the host computer, not just around the Internet. In Figure 5.1 you can see the different sorts of services that are available, some of which are just available on this host and some that entail traveling across the Internet. The / sign at the end of these gopher menu options means that selecting the option displays another menu of options.

> **News Versus Newsgroups**   Notice that one of the options is *News and Weather*. This leads to real news and weather reports, as well as *newsgroups*. You learn more about newsgroups in Lesson 10—they're known as *forums* or *discussion groups* on commercial online services. You can read peoples' messages about a particular subject, and leave your own messages. The term *news*, when used on the Internet, often refers to these groups, not to journalism.

Moving Around the Menus

Try moving around your system's menu. Notice the arrow on
the left side pointing at the selected option. Usually, at the
bottom of the menu, you'll see a summary of the keystrokes
you'll use. You may also see a way to get *Help* (in this case
you would type ?). Use this feature to see a list of keystrokes.
Experiment with all of them—you'll find a few shortcuts that
will be useful later.

These are some of the keystrokes I can use on Colorado
SuperNet's system, and which are used on many other
gopher-based systems:

Select the option the arrow points to	Right Arrow or Enter
Select an option	Type the number and press Enter
Move the arrow up the menu	Up Arrow or k
Move the arrow down the menu	Down Arrow or j
Go to the previous menu	Left Arrow or u
View the next page in long menus	Spacebar or > or + or PgDn
View the previous page in long menus	b or < or - or PgUp
Display help	?
Return to the main menu	m

Exit the menu immediately   Q
(no confirmation)

Exit the menu (the system   q
asks you to confirm)

In much of this book, I am going to explain how to use the command line to do certain things on the Internet. For instance, when I tell you how to "Telnet" or "FTP to" somewhere (don't worry about what these mean right now), I'll show you how to do it from the command line.

Remember, though, that if you have a menu system, you may be able to use the menu to carry out these operations. Spend some time figuring out what you can do, and find out how to get from the menu to the command line. Many menuing systems will do most—but not all—of what you need to do, forcing you to go to the command line for some operations.

Using the Command Line

The command line is more complicated. You have to type a command, rather than selecting from a list, so you have to remember all the commands you want to use. In Lesson 8 you read about the basics of working at the command line— creating directories, moving, copying, and deleting files, and so on. Throughout the book I'll be explaining the commands you need to use to get around the Internet from the command line.

Changing Your Password

The first thing you should do when logging onto the Internet is change your password. You don't know how many people have seen the password before or since it was given to you. Internet "break-ins" are real, and a real threat. You don't want someone reading your mail and running up your online bill, or using your account to break into the host computer and do real damage.

Changing Your Password Using the Menu

You can almost certainly find a way to change the password from the menu. In the case of Colorado SuperNet, for instance, select the *SuperNet Services* to see another menu, then select *Change Your Password*. You'll be asked to enter your current password, then have to enter the new one, twice. Because the password won't be "echoed" back to you, you won't see it on your screen when you typed it. Typing it twice ensures that you actually typed what you thought you typed.

These Things Take Time   UNIX has to check the new password before it accepts it, to make sure it's valid and not used elsewhere. So changing your password may take several minutes, depending on what else the computer is doing at the same time. If you change your password and log off and try logging back on immediately, the change may not have taken place yet. If so, use your original password again.

Changing Your Password Using the Command Line

If you want to—or have to—change the password from the command line, follow this procedure:

1. First, make sure you are at the command line (the UNIX *shell*). You should see something like this:

   teal%

   (*teal* is the name of the computer—yours is probably different—and % simply indicates that the system is waiting for you to type a command. Your system may show *$* instead of %.)

2. Type passwd and press Enter.

Be Sensitive to UNIX   You must remember
that UNIX—unlike DOS—is case-sensitive. If you
don't type commands exactly the right way, with
the correct capitalization, it won't work. If you type
PASSWD (instead of passwd) in this case, the command
will not work.

3. You are prompted to type your old password. Type
it and press Enter (you won't see what you are
typing, because the system won't "echo" it back, for
security reasons, so type carefully).

4. You're then prompted for the new password. Type
it carefully and press Enter.

5. You're prompted to type the new password again,
to make sure you typed what you thought you
typed the first time. Type it carefully and press
Enter.

Your system then tells you it's changing your password,
and returns you to the UNIX command line. Here's what the
entire procedure looks like:

```
teal% passwd
Old password:
New password:
Retype new password:
Changing password for peterk on csn.
teal%
```

Logging Off the System

To log off the system, don't just hang up your modem— your
service provider's computer will continue billing you until it
realizes that you've gone, and on some systems that might be
a long time (although most systems figure it out quite
quickly).

Logging Off Using the Menu

If you are working with a menu system, you have to type a particular character. You may have to type q, then when the system asks if you want to exit, type y. Or you may be able to type Q to close the session without the menu system asking for confirmation first.

Logging Off Using the Command Line

If you are at the UNIX shell, there are a few ways to log out, depending on the type of shell. You may be able to press Ctrl+D; type logout and press Enter; or type exit and press Enter. Or maybe any of the above. Try them all, and use the one you find easiest.

> **Fast Exits**   You can add a shortcut to your communication program. For instance, if you are using Terminal you can enter the logout command in a function button, so just clicking on the button logs you out.

Your communication program may also require you to hang up after logging out—in the case of Windows Terminal, select Hangup from the Phone menu. (Many, perhaps most, communications programs hang up your modem for you once they realize the other end has hung up.)

In this lesson you learned how to use the menu system, how to change your password, and how to log out of the system. In the next lesson, you learn about reading e-mail.

Lesson

Sending and Reading E-mail

In this lesson you learn how to read and respond to your e-mail (electronic mail).

Why E-mail?

Internet's most popular feature is its *e-mail* system. Internet provides a cheap and convenient way to send messages to friends across town, to colleagues across the world. E-mail (from the term *electronic mail*), simply means sending messages across a computer network. Instead of writing a message, placing it in an envelope, and dropping it in a mailbox, you can send the message across Internet to any user anywhere. Here are some of the advantages of e-mail:

- **Cheap** Often cheaper than mail, almost always cheaper than a phone call.

- **Fast** Much faster than mail, often taking a few seconds or minutes.

- **Convenient** No need to worry about whether the recipient is there to receive the message—they can read it later.

- **Simplifies international correspondence** No need to worry about time zones or talking with a receptionist who doesn't speak your language.

- **Mailing lists** You can create mailing lists so you can write one message but send it automatically to a group of people.

E-mail Isn't Perfect   Sometimes your e-mail goes unanswered, or even unread (and, very occasionally, undelivered). Sometimes there's no way to beat the telephone.

E-mail Addresses

In order to send someone e-mail, you need his or her *address*. An address comprises three parts—the person's *login name*, an @ sign, and the *domain*. The domain is the name by which the host computer that stores the person's mail is identified on the Internet. For instance, President Clinton's login name is, not surprisingly, *president*. The domain of the computer that sends and receives his mail is *whitehouse.gov* (the *.gov* at the end refers to government computers). So his e-mail address is *president@whitehouse.gov*.

Sorry, Wrong Address   Sometimes the address you have is not correct—some mail programs don't grab addresses correctly from incoming mail, and some don't include a full address with outgoing mail. And because the Internet is a network of networks, some member networks use different address formats. For more information, see *The Complete Idiot's Guide to the Internet*, or ask your system administrator for help.

Sending Mail to Commercial Services

Most of the large commercial online services—CompuServe, America Online, GEnie, and so on—are now connected to the Internet, so you can send mail to them. Here's how:

CompuServe   Take the CompuServe address (*61111,111* for instance), replace the comma with a period, and add *@compuserve.com* to it:

61111.111@compuserve.com

PRODIGY   Add *@prodigy.com* to the end of the Prodigy mail address.

American Online   Add *@aol.com* to the end of the America Online address.

GEnie   Add *@genie.geis.com* to the end of the GEnie address.

MCImail   Add *@mcimail.com* to the end of the MCImail address.

Using a Mail Program

Many different mail programs are available. What you have depends on which one your service provider has installed— you may even be able to choose from several. In the following examples, I'm going to use a program called Pine, one of the most popular on the Internet. In the next lesson you'll take a look at UNIX Mail, a very basic system you can use from the UNIX command line.

Getting to the Mail Reader

If you have a menu system, you should be able to get to the mail system from the menu. In Colorado SuperNet, for instance, I can select the *Mail* option and see another menu that lets me start the mail program, or select the one I want to use.

If you are starting from the command line, you can type a command to start the mail program. For instance, at Colorado SuperNet, I simply type pine and press Enter to start my mail program from the command line. (Remember that UNIX is case-sensitive. You can't type Pine or PINE.)

When Pine starts, you see something like Figure 6.1.

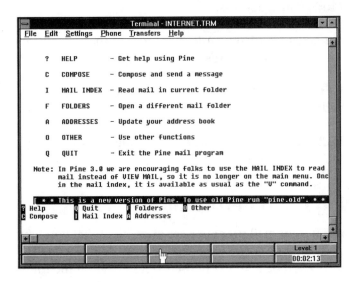

Figure 6.1   The Pine main menu.

Sending Mail

Here's how you send an e-mail message:

1. Type c (no need to press Enter). You see a blank e-mail form. (You can see a filled-in form in Figure 6.2.)

2. In the first line, type the address of the person the message is going to. While you are just learning the system, type your own address so you can then read an incoming message.

3. On the next line you can add a *Cc:* (carbon copy) *address.* The message will also be sent to this person.

4. Ignore the *Attchmnt* line for now—it's used for sending computer files along with messages, a procedure that is in its infancy on the Internet.

5. On the *Subject* line, type any kind of title for the message. (This appears in a list of messages from which the recipient can select the ones he wants to read.)

6. Then type your message, whatever you want. The message can be any length you wish. Figure 6.2 shows the e-mail message.

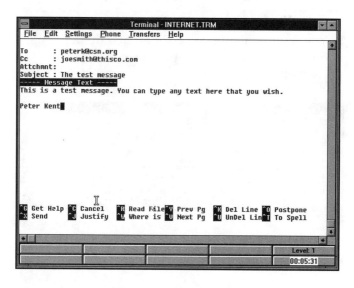

Figure 6.2 A filled-in e-mail message.

At the bottom of the screen you see a list of commands. The ^ symbol represents the *Ctrl* key—to get the help screen, for instance, you should press Ctrl+g. (Open the help screen and spend a few minutes reading, to get an idea of what you can do.)

7. To send the message, press Ctrl+x. Pine asks you to confirm that you want to send the message.

8. Type y and the message is sent.

Reading and Replying to Mail

You now find yourself back at the main menu. If you sent a message to yourself, it should arrive in a few seconds, maybe a minute or so (assuming you addressed it correctly). Pine displays a message informing you that mail has arrived. Let's view the mail, and see how to reply.

1. Press I to see a list of the mail that has arrived. You'll see something like Figure 6.3 (though it may only show one message: the one you just sent yourself).

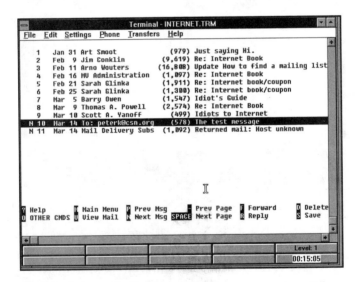

Figure 6.3 The Pine mail index.

2. If necessary, you can use the Up and Down Arrow keys to move the highlight to the message you want to read.

3. Press v or Enter to view the message. It appears in a screen like that in Figure 6.4.

4. If it's a long message, press Spacebar to move down the message a page at a time, and - (the hyphen) to move up a page at a time.

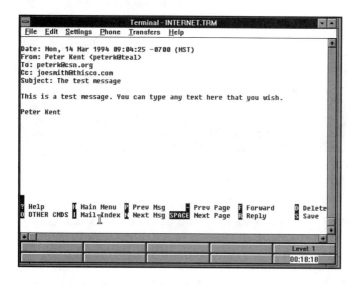

Figure 6.4 Reading mail.

5. To reply to this message, press r.

6. If this message was sent to more than one person, Pine asks you if you want to reply to all recipients. Type y to send your reply to all of them, n to reply to just the sender.

7. Pine asks if you want to include the original message in the reply. This is a common practice with e-mail, and lets you insert comments within the sender's original text. Press y. You'll see a screen like that in Figure 6.5. Notice that the text at the bottom of the message is indented with > symbols, indicating that this is the original text.

Figure 6.5 Replying to a message.

8. Type your response. You can use the Down Arrow key to move the cursor below (or within) the original text, and type there as well.

9. When you've finished, press Ctrl+x to send the reply. You'll be asked to confirm.

10. Type y and the message is sent. You return to the original message.

11. To see the next message in the list, press n.

12. To see the previous message, press p.

13. To delete the message, press d.

14. To return to the mail index (the list of messages), press i.

Pine Knows Who It's For   When replying to a message, the address of the person you are mailing to may already be filled in. If Pine recognizes that the sender has an account on the host computer (rather than being a user somewhere else), Pine simply fills in the login name and the host name.

Closing Pine

To close Pine, you must return to the main menu (Figure 6.1).

1. Press m while viewing a message or the mail index. You'll see the main menu.

2. Press q.

3. You are prompted to confirm that you want to exit. Press y.

4. If you deleted any messages while in Pine, you'll be asked to confirm that you want to remove them. Press y.

Your Mail Program

You may have Pine or something similar, or you may have a very different program. Spend some time reading the help screens and experimenting with the commands to get a feel for what you can do with mail messages. You may want to experiment by sending mail to yourself.

In this lesson you learned about the advantages of e-mail, how to send a message, and how to respond to a message. In the next lesson, you see how to use UNIX Mail.

Lesson

Working in UNIX

In this lesson you learn how to carry out basic operations at the UNIX command line.

What Is UNIX?

When you are at the UNIX command line, you are in what is known as the UNIX *shell*. You tell UNIX what to do by typing commands.

There are several different types of UNIX shell, and each one is slightly different. In general, though, most commands are the same. You probably have the C shell (the % prompt) or the Bourne shell (the $ prompt), but there are several other types.

Even if your host computer provides a menuing system, you may still have to get to the UNIX shell now and again. Some commands may not be available from the menu, and you may have to go to the shell for file management—deleting and moving files, for instance.

> **Shells** In the UNIX world, a shell is the program that produces the command line at which you type commands. In the DOS world, shell sometimes refers to graphical programs that help the user *avoid* the command line.

Getting to the Shell

How do you get to the UNIX shell? It may be all you see
when you log into your host computer. Or it may be an
option when you log in—type menu to go to the menu
system, or shell to go to the UNIX shell, for instance. Or you
may be able to get to it from a menu command. For instance,
on my host computer I can select **SuperNet Services**, then I
select **Unix Shell (Suspend Supermenu Temporarily)**.

What do you see when you get to the UNIX shell?
Something like this:

```
teal%
```

Teal is the name of my service provider's host computer, and
% is the UNIX "prompt"—the character that says, "Okay,
let's go, type something." If you are used to working on a
DOS computer, you may be used to seeing > as the prompt.
The % is the same thing. You may see a $ prompt instead,
depending on the type of UNIX shell you are using.

UNIX Directories

Like DOS, UNIX uses a directory "tree" system to organize
files. The service provider's computer stores many thousands
of computer files on a hard disk. These files can contain
words, sounds, pictures, programs, or anything else that can
be converted to a format that a computer can read.

To organize all this, we use *directories*. A *directory* is
like a box into which you can place computer files—and
more directories. A directory within a directory is called a
subdirectory.

A subdirectory can hold computer files—and more
subdirectories. It's like a filing cabinet that contains hundreds of file folders, all of which contain documents, and

many of which contain document folders. And many of those document folders contain not only documents, but smaller folders—which may also contain documents and smaller folders. We call this the *directory tree*, because it's a branching system. It makes finding and using the files on a hard disk much easier.

You will have a *home* directory on the service provider's computer. For instance, this is the *path* of my home directory:

```
/home/clients4/peterk
```

UNIX Paths Unlike in DOS, where directories in a path are separated by \ (backslash), in UNIX they are separated by / (slash).

A directory path describes how to travel along the directory tree to a particular directory. In this case, it tells us that the hard disk contains a directory named **home**. This directory contains a subdirectory called **clients4**. This subdirectory contains a subdirectory called **peterk**, my home directory. It also contains hundreds of other directories, one for each of the client accounts.

Viewing Directories

Each time you log onto a UNIX system, you are placed "in" your home directory. That is, the computer assumes you are working in the home directory, and that (for instance) new files you create will be placed there. If you transfer files from another computer using FTP (which you'll learn about in Lesson 15), they'll be placed automatically in your home directory (unless you choose another one).

To see what is in this directory, type ls (an abbreviation of "list") and press Enter. You'll see a list that looks something like this:

```
teal% ls
my.signature
network.guide
newlist.txt
s-list.txt
sig.txt
temp/
winq200a.zip
winsuper.txt
xmodem.log
teal%
```

This list shows the files and directories in your home directory. Notice the **temp/**. The / indicates that this is a directory. The others are files. Note that it doesn't show "hidden" files like .profile and so on.

Let's get some more information. Type ls -l and press Enter. Here's what you see this time:

```
teal% ls -l
-rw------- 1 peterk   258 Oct  8 12:28 my.signature
-rw------- 1 peterk 22942 Sep 30 08:05 network.guide
-rw------- 1 peterk  5972 Oct  6 13:48 newlist.txt
-rw------- 1 peterk 10985 Oct  5 08:13 s-list.txt
-rw------- 1 peterk   255 Oct  7 09:15 sig.txt
drwx------ 2 peterk   512 Oct  8 12:48 temp/
-rw------- 1 peterk 17911 Oct  8 12:29 xmodem.log
teal%
```

You can see the file or directory name on the right of each line, but there's more. Take a look at two lines:

```
drwx------ 2 peterk    512 Oct  8 12:48 temp/
-rw------- 1 peterk 282126 Oct  1 09:18 winq200a.zip
```

d or - The first character indicates whether the entry is a file or directory. A hyphen (-) means it's a file, a **d** means it's a directory.

r Means the owner of the object can read it. If he or she can't, there's a hyphen instead.

w Means the owner of the object can modify it (write). If he or she can't, there's a hyphen instead.

x Means the owner of the object can execute it—he or she can get into the directory, or execute the file (run it) if it's a program file. If the owner can do neither of these, there's a hyphen instead.

The next ten characters are related to what *other* people can do with the file, members and non-members of your *group*. (Each user on a UNIX computer is a member of a group.)

The line also shows the owner name. After the owner name you might see the group name (but not in this example). Next you see the file size, the number of bytes (characters), followed by the date and time that the file or directory was created or last modified, and, finally, the filename or directory name.

Here are a few ways to view the contents of a directory:

ls	Shows a simple list of files and directories.
ls -l	Shows the list with the file sizes and other information.
ls -al	Shows everything, including hidden files.

ls |more	Stops the list after every page (press Enter to show the next line or Spacebar to show the next page).
ls -l |more	Shows the full-information listing, broken down page by page.
dir	This is a DOS command, not UNIX, but it may be available on your system. It's the equivalent of **ls -l**.

Moving Around

When you first log on, you are in the *home* directory. This is also the *current* or *working* directory (which means the directory you are in at the moment). You can change the working directory, so you can work in a different one. To move to the previous directory in the directory tree, type cd .. and press Enter. For instance, you are in */home/clients4/username*. To move back to */home/clients4* just type cd .. and press Enter.

The cd Command Didn't Work? Note that, unlike in DOS, there must be a space between the **cd** and the **..** .

To go directly to another directory by typing cd *directoryname* and press Enter. (For instance, type cd /home/clients4/*othername* and press Enter.)

Not Sure Where You Are? Type pwd (which means "print working directory") and press Enter, and UNIX will tell you.

Creating and Removing Directories

To create a new subdirectory in the working directory, type mkdir *directoryname*. To create a subdirectory in a particular directory, type this command:

mkdir */existingdirectoryname/newdirectoryname*

To delete a directory, type rmdir *directoryname*.

Using UNIX Names

UNIX file and directory names are not like DOS names. In UNIX you can type longer names, with characters DOS won't allow you to use.

Here are a few rules:

- Names are case-sensitive—the computer regards uppercase and lowercase letters differently (unlike DOS, for instance). **FILENAME.TXT** is not the same as **filename.txt**. This is very important—you'll save hours of confusion if you remember this.

- Old versions of UNIX limited you to 14 characters in a name, but new versions have no limit.

- Don't use these characters: / | \ ! @ # $ ^ & * ( ) . Also, some UNIX versions don't like you to use **?** or — (minus sign).

- You may be able to put spaces in filenames, but don't bother, because it may upset some programs.

- UNIX doesn't have file extensions in the same way DOS does. It simply regards the period as a character like any other. You can use periods to separate words, such as *Where.can.I.find.the.source.to.C.news?.*

Case-sensitive Commands UNIX is case-sensitive in general, not just for filenames. You must type the commands correctly—you can't type **RM** if you want to delete a file (it's **rm**).

Modifying Files

Here's how to modify files:

Deleting files Use the **rm** command to delete a file—for instance:

```
rm delete.this.file
```

Moving files Use the **mv** command to move a file. Type:

```
mv filename directoryname
```

Renaming files You can also use the **mv** command to rename a file. Type:

```
mv oldfilename newfilename
```

Copying files To copy a file, use the **cp** command. For instance:

```
cp originalfilename newfilename
```

To copy the file to another directory, type:

```
cp originalfilename directoryname
```

To copy the file to another directory with a new name, use:

```
cp originalfilename directoryname/newname
```

Some Useful Commands

Here are a few more useful UNIX commands.

Repeating the last command   If you want to repeat
the command you just carried out, type !! and press
Enter. If this doesn't work, try r instead. In some shells
there is no repeat command.

Canceling what's happening   If you want to stop
what is happening, try pressing Ctrl and c at the same
time (Ctrl+c). If that doesn't help, try Ctrl+x, or q.

Finding Help   You can see instructions explaining a
command using the **man** (as in "manual") command.
Type man *commandname* | more. For instance, man
cd | more displays the help information on the **cd**
command.

In this lesson you learned the basics of working in
UNIX. In the next lesson, you learn how to find missing files,
and how to view and edit text files.

Lesson

Using UNIX Mail

In this lesson you learn how to use UNIX Mail from the command line.

What Is UNIX Mail?

UNIX Mail is a very simple program for reading and writing e-mail. It's by no means "user-friendly," but many people use it, and some even like it. You perform actions by typing commands that you have to remember—there's no command bar or menu bar to help you. Still, working with UNIX Mail can be very quick once you know what you are doing.

Sending Mail with UNIX Mail

To start UNIX Mail, you need to be at the command line. If you are using a menuing system and want to try UNIX Mail, find a menu option that will take you to the command line (the option may say **UNIX Shell**). For instance, on Colorado SuperNet you would select the SuperNet Services option, and then select the UNIX Shell option. Then follow this procedure:

1. Type mail at the command line and press Enter. You'll see an **&** sign. If there is no mail in the queue, it will say "NO MAIL FOR USERNAME" and return to the shell. You need to type mail *user@domain* in that case, where you fill in your own user name and domain in place of the italicized words.

2. Type mail, followed by the address of the person you want to send a message to, and press Enter (see Figure 8.1).

Figure 8.1 Entering a message in UNIX Mail.

3. Type a message subject and press Enter.

4. Type the message text. Unlike most other e-mail programs, UNIX Mail won't "wrap" long lines of text, so you must press Enter after every 60 characters or so.

5. When you've finished the message, press Enter, type a period (.) on a line by itself, and press Enter again.

6. You'll be prompted for a Cc: (carbon copy) address. Type the address, if any, and press Enter. UNIX Mail sends the message.

Quick Cancel To cancel a message at any time before it's sent, press Ctrl+c twice.

Viewing Messages

To view a list of messages you have received, type h and
press Enter. You'll see the first 20 messages, something like
Figure 8.2. If you have more than 20 messages, press z and
Enter to view the next screenful, and -z and Enter to see the
last screenful.

```
                        Terminal - INTERNET.TRM
 File   Edit  Settings  Phone  Transfers  Help

& h
>   1 aesmoot@aescon.com Mon Jan 31 11:25   29/1036  Just saying Hi.
    2 CONKLIN@BITNIC.EDUCOM.EDU Wed Feb  9 09:06  230/9472  Re: Internet Boo
    3 Arno.Wouters@phil.ruu.nl Sat Feb 12 01:53  417/16473 Update How to Fin
mail
    4 mv-admin@mv.MV.COM Tue Feb 15 23:33   41/1132  Re: Internet Book
    5 glinka@ans.net     Mon Feb 21 14:13   80/1903  Re: Internet book/coupo
    6 glinka@ans.net     Fri Feb 25 06:53   43/1329  Re: Internet book/coupo
    7 bowen              Sat Mar  5 09:04   43/1567  Idiot's Guide
    8 tpowell@CERF.NET   Wed Mar  9 16:36   72/2576  Re: Internet Book
    9 yanoff@csd4.csd.uwm.edu Thu Mar 10 22:40   19/561   Idiots to Internet
   10 peterk             Mon Mar 14 09:11   22/620   The test message
   11 MAILER-DAEMON      Mon Mar 14 09:11   35/1128  Returned mail: Host unk
 U 12 peterk             Mon Mar 14 09:33   32/682   Re: The test message
 N 13 peterk             Mon Mar 14 10:03   13/495   Another test message
 N 14 peterk             Mon Mar 14 10:05   15/500   Another test
 N 15 MAILER-DAEMON      Mon Mar 14 10:05   28/1013  Returned mail: Host unk
&

                                                        Level: 1
                                                        01:22:29
```

Figure 8.2 Viewing a list of messages.

This shows you the message number (its position in the
list), the sender, the date and time it was received, the
number of lines and characters in the message, and the
subject. In the left column you also see characters that
indicate the status of the information:

U Unread—the message was in the inbox last time
you looked, but you haven't read it yet.

N New—the message has arrived since the last time
you checked your mail.

P   Preserved—you've told UNIX Mail not to remove this message from the inbox when you close the program (this is done by typing pre *message number*). When you close, UNIX Mail moves the messages you've read to a file called *mbox*. (If you see other messages that are still in the list but have apparently been read, they were read with a different mail program.)

>   Indicates the current message, the one that any commands you use will work on. (For instance, pressing Enter displays the current message.)

Reading a Message

If you want to read a message, type the number of the message and press Enter. If the > sign is pointing at the message you want to read, just press Enter.

If the message is short, you can read it. Unfortunately, if it's *not* short, it flies past so quickly you won't be able to read it. You can save it in a file and read it later, or read it in a text editor.

> **Scroll Stopper**   If the message is very long—not uncommon on the Internet—you can stop it scrolling across your screen by typing Ctrl+c or Ctrl+x.

Reading in a Text Editor

To put a message in the text editor, where you can read it, type e *number* and press Enter. The message appears in whatever text editor you've set as your default. (*Before* you use the text editor, you should probably ask your system

administrator what text editor is installed as the default, and
how to exit from the editor. You may have several editors
you can choose from.)

If you find yourself in vi, a basic text editor with ~
symbols down one side, press Esc three times, type :q! and
press Enter to quit without saving changes. Other text
editors may display a list of commands that you can use.

> **Which Editor?**   To change your default editor,
> see Lesson 9.

Reading Messages in Text Files

To save a message—or several—in a text file, type s *numbers filename* and press Enter. For instance, typing s 1-4
newmailfile.txt would save messages 1 to 4 in a file called
newmailfile.txt. (Which is not the same as
NEWMAILFILE.TXT, remember, as UNIX is case-sensitive—
and notice that UNIX allows long filenames.)

Later, when you've closed UNIX Mail, you can read
your mail messages. Type more *filename* and press Enter
(more newmailfile.txt, in this case). You'll see your messages
page by page—press Spacebar to move down a page. Press
Ctrl+c to stop viewing the file.

Replying to Mail

Here's how to reply to a mail message in UNIX Mail.

1. Type r *number* and press Enter. For instance, to
   reply to message 14, type r 14 and press Enter.

2. The address and subject lines of the message will
   already be filled in. Type your reply.

3. Type the message text. Remember to press Enter after every 60 characters or so.

4. When you've finished the message, press Enter, type a period (.), and press Enter again.

5. You'll be prompted for a Cc: (carbon copy) address. Type the address, if any, and press Enter. UNIX Mail sends the message.

Quoting the Original Message

In the last lesson, you saw how the Pine mail program could enter the original message text in the reply. UNIX Mail doesn't do this directly, but there is a way to force it to do so.

When you are entering the text of your reply, type ~f *number* and press Enter (where *number* is the message number you are replying to). The ~ must be in the first column of a line, and the command must sit on the line by itself. This tells UNIX Mail to insert that message into the text of the message you are writing.

Forwarding a Message You can also use the ~f *number* command to forward a message, not just reply to one. Use the mail command to write a new message, and use the ~f *number* command to insert a received message into one you are writing.

Deleting Messages

To delete a message, type d *number*. For instance, type d 5 to delete message 5, d 5-7 to delete messages 5 to 7. UNIX Mail removes these messages when you close the program, and doesn't copy them to the *mbox* file (messages that you read in UNIX Mail but *don't* delete are moved to the *mbox* file).

To *undelete* a message—bring it back if you accidentally delete it—type u *number*.

Closing UNIX Mail

When you've finished working with UNIX Mail, type q and press Enter. UNIX Mail closes, and any messages you've just read are placed in a text file called *mbox*, and removed from the UNIX Mail "inbox"—you won't see them next time you enter UNIX Mail.

If you want to close UNIX Mail—but stop it from moving messages to the *mbox* file—type x and press Enter.

In this lesson you learned how to work with UNIX Mail. In the next lesson, you learn how to work at the UNIX command line.

Lesson

Finding, Viewing, and Editing Files

In this lesson you find out how to use UNIX commands to find a missing file, and to view and edit text files. You also find out how to create a signature file to attach to your mail messages.

Finding Lost Files

If you know the name of the file you want, but aren't sure where it is, type find . -name *filename* -print and press Enter. If the file is in the working directory, the one you are in when you use the command, UNIX simply repeats the name to you (like this: **./filename**). If it's in another directory, UNIX shows you which one (like this: **./directoryname/ filename**).

The **find** command only searches through the working directory and its subdirectories (and their subdirectories); it doesn't go the *other* way, and search the directory of which the working directory is a subdirectory. And remember, make sure you type the name correctly, with each letter in the correct case. If you are looking for **Lost.File**, you can't type lost.file and expect it to work.

Viewing Files

You will occasionally want to view the contents of text files. There are a couple of quick ways to do so. If it's a short file, type cat *filename*, press Enter, and the file is displayed on your screen. If it's long, type more *filename*, and it is displayed page by page; press Spacebar to see the next page, or Enter to move line by line. And press q to stop viewing the file.

You can also view a text file by placing it in a text editor, where you can move up and down in the document, and make changes.

Which Text Editor?

A *text editor* is a program that lets you view the contents of a text file and make changes to it. Unlike a word processor, a text editor doesn't make many formatting changes to the file. While word processors can add different types of character style (bold or italic, for instance), use different fonts, arrange margins and columns, and so on, a text editor lets you type words but not format the text.

Default Text Editor

You may have several text editors available to you, but you already have one set up as a default for use in UNIX Mail (as you saw in Lesson 7), and various other programs. (The default editor appears automatically in UNIX Mail when you use the **e number** command.)

To find out which editor is set as the default, type setenv at the UNIX shell and press Enter. You see a long list of "environment" information: your home directory, the type of UNIX shell you are using (for instance, *csh* means the C shell), and other items. One of them will be something like this: *EDITOR=/usr/local/bin/pico*. This shows the directory in which the editor is stored, and the type of editor. In this case, the *pico* editor is being used.

You can change the editor by typing this command: setenv EDITOR *editorname* and press Enter. For instance, if you want to use pico, type setenv EDITOR pico and press Enter.

Pick an Editor   Ask your system administrator which text editors are available, then try them all to find the one that is easiest. Some are pretty clunky.

Viewing Files in a Text Editor

Let's take a quick look at pico, one of the easier text editors (and available on many systems). To start pico and load a text file into it—perhaps a file you saved from the mail system—type pico *filename* at the UNIX shell, and press Enter. For instance, to open a file called *todays-mail*, you would type pico todays-mail and press Enter.

That's pico, not PICO   Make sure you type pico in all lowercase, including the p. It won't work if you use uppercase.

You'll see a screen similar to that in Figure 9.1.

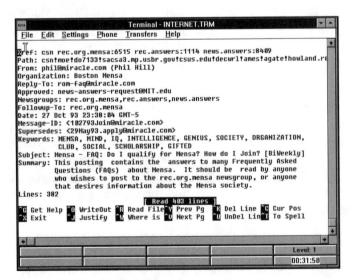

Figure 9.1   The pico text editor.

You can now move around in this file, using Ctrl+v and Ctrl+y to move down the text and back up the text. You can also use the arrow keys to move the cursor around in the file, and even use Ctrl+w to search for a particular word. This is a lot easier than using the **cat** or **more** commands to read a file—with those commands there's no way to move back up the file; you have to start over.

When you've finished reading the file, press Ctrl+x to close pico.

Creating a Signature File

Let's take a look at how to use the text editor to create a signature file. Most e-mail programs automatically append the signature file to the end of your e-mail (with UNIX Mail you have to use the **~r filename** command to tell the system to add the file).

Signature File   A *signature file* contains information about you—anything you want other people to see. You might include your full name and address, along with your e-mail address and telephone numbers. Some people include a line or two explaining their profession or business.

Keep It Short and Sweet   Don't get carried away with the signature file—if you put too much into it you'll irritate other users. Internet "etiquette" demands that you don't waste too many system "resources" with huge signature files, and that you advertise your business very subtly.

The signature file is a hidden text file called *.signature* in your home directory. Here's how you can create one:

1. At the UNIX shell, type pico .signature. pico opens, with a blank screen.

2. Type what you would like to appear in your signature file. Use the arrow keys to move around, and Backspace to delete characters. (See Figure 9.2.)

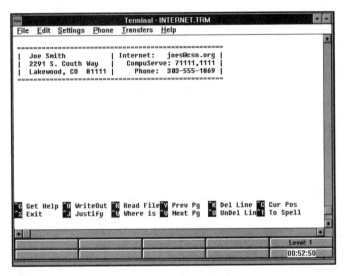

Figure 9.2   Creating a signature file in pico.

3. When you're finished, press Ctrl+x. pico displays this prompt:

```
Modified buffer: Save before leaving (y/n)?
```

4. Type y and press Enter. pico closes, and your file is saved.

Now, whenever you use a mail program to create a mail message (with the exception of UNIX Mail), the text you entered will be placed at the bottom of the message automatically.

In this lesson you learned how to find missing files, display files in a text editor, and use a text editor to create a signature file. In the next lesson, you learn about the Internet's newsgroups.

Working with Newsgroups

In this lesson you learn how to read messages and leave messages in the Internet newsgroups.

What Is a Newsgroup?

If you've used any other on-line information services, you may be familiar with terms such as *forums*, *message boards*, or *discussion groups*. These are "areas" in which you can read messages about a particular interest. They provide a great way to meet other people interested in the same subjects as you, whether personal or professional. On the Internet these areas are known as *newsgroups*, and there are thousands of them.

Here's how it works: for just about any subject, there's a newsgroup. The system administrator "subscribes" to various groups, maybe a few hundred, maybe a few thousand. Every system that subscribes to a particular newsgroup periodically gets an update of the newsgroup's messages. You can read messages that your system has subscribed to, and you can send messages to the newsgroup.

What Can a Newsgroup Do for You?

For just about any subject, there's a newsgroup somewhere. There are groups on military science, skydiving, cooking with sourdough, politics, British comedy, anthropology, nuclear physics, telephone sex, Kristi Yamaguchi, supermodels—you name it, there's probably a newsgroup for it. There's even a newsgroup about stupid newsgroups.

news.announce.newusers Subscribe to this newsgroup. There are four messages posted to this newsgroup that contain short descriptions of thousands of different newsgroups—they'll help you track down the ones that interest you.

You won't necessarily have access to all the newsgroups, but if you hear about one you'd like to use, you can ask your system administrator to subscribe. Ask your system administrator for a list of newsgroups the system has available to you. There's probably a file on-line somewhere that lists them.

Getting to a Newsgroup

Messages from newsgroups are stored somewhere on the host computer as text files. You could, if you wished, read the text file itself, but this is not a very efficient way to do it. Instead, there are *newsreaders*, programs that help you find your way through a newsgroup.

You start the newsreader from the menu system, or by typing a command at the UNIX shell. Ask your system administrator which newsreaders are available, and how to get to them. You may have programs such as *tin*, *nn*, *trn*, and *rn* available.

For instance, I can start my newsreaders by selecting News and Weather to see a menu that lets me select a reader, post messages to a newsgroup, and read newsgroup messages. If I'm at the command prompt, I can just start a reader by typing its name and pressing Enter.

Reading Newsgroup Messages

Let's see an example of working with newsgroups. I'm going to use rn as an example. It's one of the most commonly used readers, and it's similar to another popular reader, nn. However, it's by no means the best; ask your service provider what's available, and try each one. The following description will help you use rn, if that's what you have, or at least give you an idea of what the other systems can do.

The first time you use rn, you'll probably see a short introduction, which tells you that

- To enter a command, you just type the appropriate letter—you don't need to press Enter.

- To see a list of commands, type h. This shows the commands appropriate for your current location in the newsreader.

- You can press Spacebar to tell rn to carry out the "default" command; normally the "yes" response is the default.

Listing the New Newsgroups

When you continue, rn may show you a list of new newsgroups, newsgroups that the system administrator has just recently subscribed to. As it names each one, you can decide what you want to do with the group. For instance:

```
Newsgroup zer.z-netz.wissenschaft.physik not
in .newsrc—subscribe? [ynYN]
```

This is telling you that the newsgroup *zer.z-netz.wissenschaft.physik* has been added by your service provider, and that it doesn't appear in the .newsrc file.

.newsrc The .newsrc file is a hidden file in your home directory that lists all the newsgroups you have subscribed to. When you first use a newsreader, you may find that your system administrator has already subscribed to a variety of newsgroups for you.

You can type y, n, Y, or N:

y   to subscribe to the new group

Y   to subscribe to *all* the new groups

n   to *not* subscribe to the new group

N   to *not* subscribe to any of the new groups

If you do decide to subscribe to a group, rn will ask you where you want to put the group: at the top of the list (type ^), at the bottom of the list ($), before a named newsgroup (*-name*), after a named newsgroup (*+name*), or in a particular position (type the position number). If you're not sure where to put it, you can type L to see a list of the newsgroups and their numbers. Its position will affect the sequence in which the newsgroups are presented to you when you start your newsreader.

Listing the Subscribed Newsgroups

When you've finished with the new groups, rn will show a list of your subscribed groups, and tell you how many unread messages each has.

You'll see something like this:

```
Unread news in alt.sex.wizards
1230 articles
Unread news in alt.silly.group.names.d
3 articles
Unread news in alt.society.revolution
55 articles
Unread news in bit.listserv.scuba-l
823 articles
Unread news in soc.culture.yugoslavia
1793 articles
etc.
******** 1230 unread articles in
alt.sex.wizards—read now? [ynq]
```

The "etc." means there are more newsgroups than shown in this list. If you want to read the first article (message) in this newsgroup, press y. Otherwise, press n to go to the next group with unread messages.

> **Articles**   Newsgroup messages are commonly known as *articles*, or *postings*.

There are some other options:

- Unsubscribe from this group—Type u.

- List the articles in the newsgroup—Type =.

- Go to the next group even if it has no unread messages—Type N.

Reading Newsgroup Messages

Take a look at the first unread article in a newsgroup. Just type y at one of the *read now?* prompts. You'll see something like Figure 10.1.

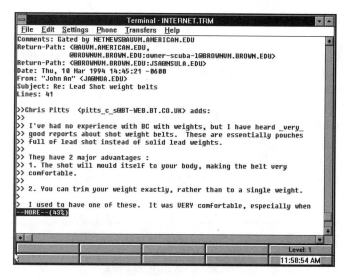

Figure 10.1   The rn newsreader.

The first part of the message is the usual header stuff—you can see the article number and newsgroup name, address of the person who sent it, the Subject title, and the date. You can generally ignore the rest of the header. It shows how the message got to the newsgroup.

Working with Newsgroup Messages

What now? Here are a few things you may want to do:

Unsubscribe   You weren't sure what the newsgroup was all about, but now that you've seen it, you know you don't want it. Type **u** to "unsubscribe," so you won't come to this group next time.

Read the rest of the message   Press Spacebar to read the rest of the message (or Enter to see the next line). If you're at the end of a message and press Spacebar, you'll move directly to the next one. You can move back up one page by pressing b, or to the top of the message by pressing Ctrl+r.

Go to another article   Press N to go to the next
article, or n to go to the next *unread* article. (This is
the same thing when you first start. Your newsreader
knows which messages you have seen, and assumes
you've *read* them. As you view each one, it's *marked*
as read.) Press Ctrl+N to go to the next unread article
with the same subject (articles that are replies to other
articles). To go the other way—backwards—substitute
P. That is, P for the previous article, p for the previous
unread article, or Ctrl+P to go to the previous unread
article with the same subject.

Viewing a List

You can save a lot of time by avoiding messages in which
you have no interest—simply select the ones you want to see
from a list. Press = to see a list of the unread articles:

```
3167 Re: New free dive record
3168 Re: Definition of Curmudgeon
3169 Re: catching tropical fish
3170 NED =
3171 Re: catching tropical fish
3172 Re: goodbye !!!
3173 Definition of Curmudgeon
3174 Re: Sea of Cortez Video
3175 NO SUBJECT
3176 The pros and cons of shrimpin
```

You'll see a screenful of subjects at a time—press
Spacebar to see more. Unfortunately, rn doesn't let you
select by highlighting a message in the list (some other
newsreaders do). Still, it shows the message numbers, so you
can type a number and press Enter to go right to a particular
message.

Notice, by the way, that some message titles start with
Re:. This means that they are replies to another message.

Going to Another Newsgroup

To leave a newsgroup, press q once to quit the message you're in, then press q again to return to the newsgroups list—rn will show you the name of the next group in sequence, and ask if you want to read its messages.

Replying to Newsgroup Articles

To reply to a newsgroup article in rn, simply press f (or F to include the original article in the response). If you want to respond via e-mail, rather than writing a public message in the newsgroup, press r (or R to include the original article in the response).

Either way, you'll see a series of prompts that lead you through the procedure for creating a message using your default text editor. (You learned how to define the default editor in Lesson 9.)

Starting a New Discussion

If you want to start a new topic in a newsgroup, you have to leave rn to do it. More sophisticated newsreaders let you send a new article—rather than a response—directly from the reader, but rn won't. Instead, you might have to use the Pnews program, or perhaps select a menu option—in Colorado SuperNet, for instance, there's a *Post to Usenet Newsgroup* option.

In this lesson you learned how to read and respond to newsgroup messages. In the next lesson, you learn about another type of message "forum," the LISTSERV mailing lists.

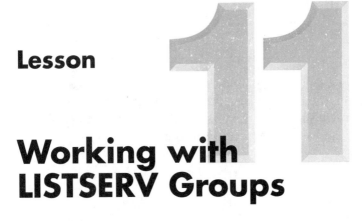

Lesson

Working with LISTSERV Groups

In this lesson you learn how to use the LISTSERV groups, discussion groups based on the e-mail system.

What Is LISTSERV?

LISTSERV groups are similar to newsgroups in that they are discussion groups—people exchanging information about many different subjects. But they work in a completely different way—they use the Internet e-mail system to exchange messages.

When you subscribe to a LISTSERV group, you are adding your name to a mailing list. Each time someone sends a message to the group, the message is automatically forwarded to everyone on the mailing list, arriving as e-mail.

There are 4,000 or more of these groups, as diverse as CHRISTIA@FINHUTC (a Christian discussion group), ISO8859@JHUVM (a group that discusses "ASCII/EBCDIC-character set" issues), L-HCAP@NDSUVM1 (a group for people interested in issues related to handicapped people in education), and PHILOSOP@YORKVM1 (the Philosophy Discussion Forum).

Although many of the LISTSERV groups are of a technical nature, you'll also find groups run by the African-American Student Network, the American Association of

Teachers of German, and the Forum da Associacao Brasileira de Estatistica, and covering subjects such as Chinese music, Dungeons and Dragons, American dialects, and agriculture.

The LISTSERV Address

Let's take a look at the LISTSERV address. It's made up of three parts: the group name itself, the LISTSERV *site*, and **.bitnet**. For instance, the address of the group College Activism/Information List is **actnow-l@brownvm.bitnet**. "Actnow-l" is the name of the group, and "brownvm.bitnet" is the name of the site.

A *site* is a computer that has the LISTSERV program and handles one or more LISTSERV groups. A site may have dozens of groups. The brownvm site, for instance, also has the ACH-EC-L, AFRICA-L, and AGING-L forums, among about 70 others.

Finding a List of LISTSERV Groups

If you want to find a list of LISTSERV groups, send an e-mail message to listserv@bitnic.educom.edu. In the *body* of the message (not the subject) write list global. That's all you need. You'll automatically get an e-mail message containing a large list of LISTSERV groups, with a short (less than one line) description of each one.

> **Peered**   Some groups are listed as *peered*. A *peered* LISTSERV group is the same as a *moderated* newsgroup—someone's checking the mail and deciding what stays and what's trashed.

Subscribing to the LISTSERV Group

Once you've found a LISTSERV group to which you want to subscribe, you must send an e-mail message to the LISTSERV site (not to the group itself), asking to subscribe to the list. You'll send a message with the following text in the *body* of the message (not the subject).

SUBSCRIBE *group firstname lastname*

For instance, I found this group in the LISTSERV list:

```
CRUISE-L@UNLVM 'Cruising The Internet'
Information List
```

CRUISE-L is the name of the group, UNLVM is the LISTSERV site. To subscribe to this group, I could use UNIX Mail to send an e-mail message like this (boldface indicates what I would type; you can use any mail program you wish):

```
teal% mail listserv@unlvm.bitnet
Subject:
SUBSCRIBE cruise-l Peter Kent
.
Cc:
teal%
```

Notice that you send the message to listserv@*sitename*.bitnet, and that the SUBSCRIBE message contains only the name of the group, not the entire group address.

You may (or may not) receive some kind of confirmation message from the group, telling you that you have subscribed and providing background information about the group (as well as the different commands you can use).

Once you have subscribed, just sit back and wait for the messages to arrive. Or send your own—simply address mail to the full group address, in the preceding case to cruise-l@unlvm.bitnet.

"Unsubscribing" From a Group

When you're tired of receiving all these messages, you have to unsubscribe. Send another message to the LISTSERV address. This time it looks like this:

```
teal% mail listserv@unlvm.bitnet
Subject:
SIGNOFF cruise-1
.
Cc:
teal%
```

Again, make sure you address it to listserv@, not the group name itself. And make sure the group name appears after signoff, but not the entire group address.

Advanced LISTSERV

There are a few neat things you can do with LISTSERV. By sending e-mail messages to the LISTSERV site, you can tell the LISTSERV software how you want to handle your messages. You'll probably receive an information message when you subscribe, describing the available features and how to find more information.

You can ask LISTSERV to send you an acknowledgment each time you send a message (most groups *won't* do this, by default). You can find information about another group member—or tell LISTSERV not to provide information about you to other users. You can tell LISTSERV to stop sending you messages temporarily—perhaps when you go on vacation—and tell it to send only the message subjects, rather than the entire messages. You can request a specific message, and even search the archives for old messages.

Finding LISTSERV Information

When using these special features or asking for information, you send mail to the listserv@*sitename*.bitnet address. Here's an example of how you can combine several commands, and find more information. For instance:

```
teal% mail listserv@unlvm.bitnet
Subject:
list
query cruise-l
info refcard
.
Cc:
teal%
```

This tells LISTSERV to send you a list of the groups handled by this site (list), tells you what options you have set (query cruise-l), and sends you a reference guide (info refcard). It's also a good idea to use the info ? command to find out what user documentation they have available, then use the info *documentname* command to get the site to send you specific documents.

> **Sending to the Group** Are you getting complaints from the LISTSERV site and other group members? Remember that to send a message to be read by group members, you must address it to groupname@*sitename*.bitnet. For all other purposes—to subscribe, unsubscribe, change user options, get more information, and so on—send the message to listserv@*sitename*.bitnet.

In this lesson you learned how to send and receive messages from LISTSERV groups. In the next lesson, you learn how to use Gopher to get around the Internet.

Lesson

Using Gopher

In this lesson you learn how to use Gopher, one of the easiest ways to find your way around the Internet.

What Is *Gopher*?

Gopher is a menu system that helps you move around the Internet. The Gopher system comprises several hundred Gopher *servers*—computers that contain indexes—and thousands of Gopher clients—computers running the Gopher menu software that accesses the servers' indexes.

All servers are public, so any client can access the information from any server. When you start the Gopher menu, the software goes out onto the network and grabs all the information it needs from one of the servers.

Gopher Gopher was developed at the University of Minnesota—home of the "Golden Gophers." "Gofer" is slang for someone who "goes fer" things. And the system digs its way through the Internet, like a gopher in a burrow. When using Gopher you are traveling through *Gopherspace*.

Which Gopher Will You Use?

Which Gopher client are you going to use? You have a few options:

- **Perhaps your service provider's system is based on Gopher.** Some service providers have based their own user interface on the Gopher system. The menu system used by Colorado SuperNet that we looked at in Lesson 4—shown again in Figure 12.1—is one of these.

- **You might be able to run Gopher from the UNIX prompt.** While you may not see the Gopher menu when you log in, it may be available when you type gopher and press Enter at the UNIX shell.

- **You might be able to telnet to a Gopher site.** Some computers let you login on a *telnet* connection and use their Gopher system, though this method is falling out of favor.

Telnet   *Telnet* is a system that lets you log onto another computer on the Internet, whether in the same city or on another continent. You learn more about telnet in Lesson 14.

Using Your Service Provider's Gopher

Most Internet users work with their service provider's own Gopher, the one already installed on their systems. When you log in, you may find you are already in Gopher—if you find yourself in a menu system that looks like that in Figure 12.1, there's a good chance you are in a Gopher: .

Gopher Types   Your Gopher may look different. The one I'm using—the Curses Gopher—is the most common, but there are others. Commands vary, but the principles are the same.

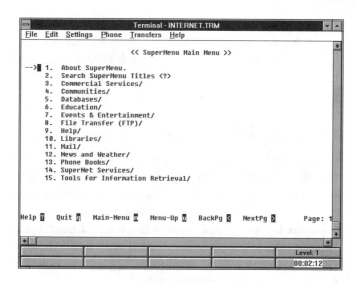

Figure 12.1   A Gopher menu.

Notice that some of the menu options have a slash (/) at the end. This is a typical Gopher indication that selecting that option leads to another menu, a sub-menu. Notice also the commands at the bottom. These are typical Gopher menu commands. And there's even an "About" option right at the top—if you select this option, at least on this particular system, you'd find that this is, indeed, a Gopher system.

Starting From the UNIX Shell

If you don't see a Gopher menu when you log in, you may be able to start Gopher from the system prompt (the UNIX shell if you are working on a UNIX host). Simply type gopher and press Enter. Hopefully your service provider has set up a Gopher client—he will have defined the Gopher command that builds the Gopher menu for you. Again, you'll see something similar to the menu we just looked at.

Maybe your service provider does it differently—you might have to select a command from a different menu system. If you can't find Gopher, ask your service provider how to get to it, or check the documentation you got with your account.

Using Gopher Through Telnet

It's possible that your system administrator hasn't set up Gopher. If not, ask if he could do so. In the meantime, see if you can use someone else's Gopher. You can *telnet* to another computer, and use Gopher from there. However, with the incredible increase in Internet traffic in the past year or two it's becoming more difficult to do this—some Gopher sites that used to allow public access now limit Gopher use to their own accounts.

Still, if you want to try it, you can try these sites (they may not all work):

consultant.micro.umn.edu   Log in as gopher. (This is the University of Minnesota, the home of the Gopher.)

hafnhaf.micro.umn.edu   Log in as gopher. (This is the University of Minnesota again.)

library.wustl.edu   No login required (Washington University, St. Louis, MO).

ux1.cso.uiuc.edu   Log in as gopher (University of Illinois).

panda.uiowa.edu   No login required (University of Iowa).

gopher.sunet.se   Log in as gopher. (This is in Sweden, but the menus are in English.)

info.anu.edu.au   Log in as info (Australia).

gopher.chalmers.se   Log in as gopher. (This is in Sweden, and the menus are in Swedish and English. Confusing if you don't speak Swedish, because the Swedish comes first.)

tolten.puc.cl   Log in as gopher then press Enter. (This is in Chile, and it's mainly in Spanish, with a little English.)

To telnet to a Gopher site, use this procedure:

1. At the UNIX prompt, type telnet *sitename* and press Enter. For instance, to telnet to **consultant.micro.umn.edu** type telnet consultant.micro.umn.edu and press Enter.

2. When you see a Login: prompt, type the necessary login name (see the list above) and press Enter.

3. If the system asks for a password, type your e-mail address.

4. If you see a prompt like this: TERM=(vt100), press Enter or type the name of the terminal type you are using and press Enter.

Using Gopher

Use one of the methods just described to get to a Gopher menu. Below the menu's title line are the menu options, each one numbered. You can type the number you want to select, or move the arrow to it and press Enter or the right arrow to select it. Move the arrow using your keyboard's up and down arrow keys, or, if they won't work, the j and k keys. Here are some other commands you'll need:

Return to the previous menu	u or left arrow
Return to the main menu	m

View the next page in or PgDn long menus	Spacebar or > or +
View the previous page in long menus	b or < or - or PgUp
Exit Gopher (the system will ask you to confirm)	q
Exit Gopher immediately (no confirmation)	Q

Play with these commands for a few minutes and you'll soon get the hang of it. Spend some time experimenting and following the different menu options to wherever they lead.

Don't Press Enter   While working in the Gopher menus, you don't need to press Enter to carry out a command (unless told to do so). For instance, to go to the previous menu simply press u. No need to press Enter after the u.

Slow Response?   If you telnet to a Gopher, you may find the system responds very slowly, because such Gophers are often very heavily used.

Menu Indicators

Each menu option has some kind of symbol or word at the end. Here are the most common:

| / | Selecting the menu option displays another menu—the menu option is, in effect, a "directory." |
| <?> | Select this and you can enter a search word. |

. (period)	Select this and the Gopher displays a document.
<TEL>	Selecting this to telnet to another computer system.
<bin> or **<PC Bin>**	Leads to a DOS file that has been compressed with an archive program such as PKZIP.
<Movie>	Leads to a video file.
<Picture>	Leads to a graphics file.
<HQX>	Leads to a BinHex file, a Macintosh file that has been converted to ASCII so it can be transferred as e-mail.

Option Details

You can find more detailed information about a menu option by moving the arrow next to the item and pressing =. You'll see a list of information, including the type number, and the path showing where the data is stored—which computer and which directory on the computer.

These are the type numbers you may see:

0	A text file.
1	A directory; that is, selecting this option leads to another menu.
2	A "phonebook" you can use to find Internet users.
4	A BinHex Macintosh file.
5	A DOS compressed file, such as a ZIP or ARC file.
6	A UUENCODed file. You'll need UUDECODE to convert the file to its original format.
7	Select this option and you'll be prompted to enter a search word.

8	This menu option takes you to a telnet session.
9	Select this option and you'll be sent a binary file—you don't necessarily want to do this, unless your system is set up to receive such a file.
T	This menu option takes you to a tn3270 connection (an IBM 3270 equivalent of the telnet session.)
s	A sound file.
g	A GIF graphics file.
M	A MIME e-mail file-transfer format file.

Some advanced Gopher clients have "viewers" that can accept the more unusual types of data. A client may have a GIF viewer, so if you select a GIF graphics file you'll actually be able to see the picture on your screen. The basic "Curses" Gopher client cannot do that.

> **Don't Use Some Menu Options**   Do not try to select data types—such as sound or graphics—that your Gopher client cannot handle. (The simple Curses Gopher cannot "view" anything but text files.) At best it's a waste of time. At worst your computer may crash.

In this lesson you learned how to use a Gopher to find your way around the Internet. In the next lesson, you learn how to save what you find, and how to customize your Gopher using Bookmarks and Veronica.

Lesson

More on Gopher

*In this lesson you learn how to save documents and files
that you find in a Gopher menu, how to search a Gopher
menu, and how to "customize" it using bookmarks and
Veronica.*

Saving What You Find

You can save files and documents in different ways, depending on where the client you are using is on the Internet.

If you are using a client on your service provider's
computer, you can save things on your service provider's
computer. If you are using a telnet Gopher session, your
options are more limited. I assume you are working with
your own (or your service provider's) Gopher, so some of
what I describe next won't work if you are telnetting.

Saving a Document

If you are using your service provider's Gopher, there are
several ways to save a document. First, you can save it while
you are reading it. Press q and then s and you'll see something like Figure 13.1. (In some cases, typing q takes you
back to the menu. You can save from there—as you'll see in
a moment—or you can return to the document and press s
without pressing q first.)

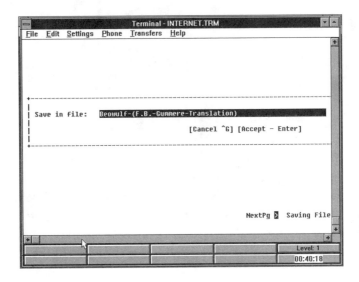

Figure 13.1   Saving a file.

Press Enter and that's it—you've saved the file (it's in your home directory if you are working with your service provider's Gopher client).

Save From the Menu   You can use this method at the menu itself—just place the arrow (—>) next to the menu option, and press s. (Remember that menu options that end with a period are documents).

If you are working on a dial-in terminal connection with your service provider's Gopher client, you may want to send the data back to your own computer. Type D to see something like Figure 13.2.

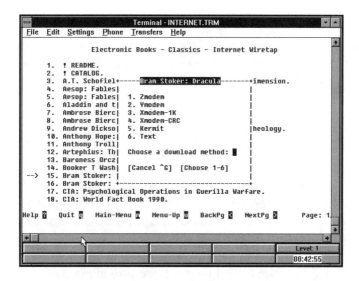

Figure 13.2 Downloading to your computer.

Menu Option Disappears You tried to download a file, but the menu option disappeared! You probably pressed d instead of D. The d command removes menu options. To get the menu option back, you have to go back one menu (u) and then return (Enter). (If you remove that line from the main menu, though, you'll have to leave the Gopher client and restart it.)

You can type the number associated with the type of file transfer you've got your communications program set to, and away you go. In the case of Zmodem, your program starts automatically for you—assuming the program has Zmodem—in other cases, you have to tell it to begin (see Lesson 17 for more information about file transfers). When the transfer is finished, press Enter to return to the Gopher menu.

Saving Files

In some cases you can use Gopher in place of FTP to transfer files across the world. (If you telnet to a Gopher client, you won't be able to do this.)

> **FTP** FTP means File Transfer Protocol, a way to transfer files between computers. See Lesson 15.
>
> Plain English

The procedures are similar to those used for grabbing text files. Simply select the menu option that leads to the file by typing its number and pressing Enter or by placing the arrow next to it and pressing Enter or s. (You'll see the same Save in File box we looked at a moment ago.) This will save the file on your service provider's computer. If you are using a dial-in connection, and want to transfer the file directly back to your own computer, place the arrow next to the menu option, and press D to download.

Searching for Entries

Some Gopher menus are very long. You can search for a particular menu option by pressing / and then typing the word you are looking for. You'll see something like Figure 13.3.

When you press Enter, you move to the first entry that matches what you typed; you can press n to move to the next matching entry. In the example, we are searching for books by Darwin.

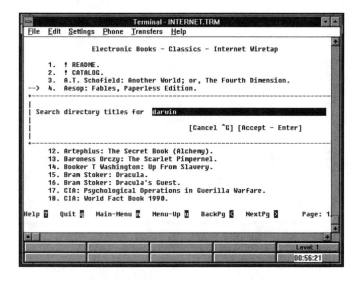

Figure 13.3   Searching a menu.

Create Your Own Menu— Placing Bookmarks

While you're working in the Gopher, you might want to place "bookmarks." These let you create a list of menu options in which you are interested—you can travel around, marking the things you think you may want to check into further, then come back and examine each, one at a time.

Use these commands:

Add the selected menu item to the bookmark list	a
Add the current menu to the bookmark list	A

| View the list of bookmarks | v |
| Delete a bookmark from the list | d |

For instance, suppose you find something you want to mark, and you press a. You'll see something like Figure 13.4.

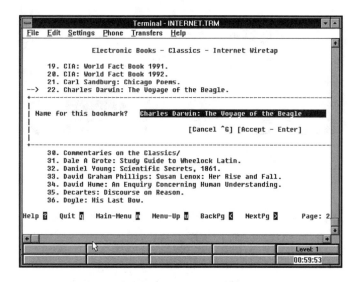

Figure 13.4 Placing a Bookmark.

Press Enter to place the bookmark. Or press Ctrl+u, type a different name, then press Enter.

Later, when you want to view all the bookmarks, just press v. You'll see something like Figure 13.5.

This is just like any other Gopher menu—you select items in the same way—but it's a menu that you created.

If you are using a Gopher that you telnetted to, these bookmarks will be lost when you leave the system. If you are using your service provider's system the bookmarks will be saved, which is very convenient. In effect, you can build

your own menu of frequently used menu options, and view
the menu at any time by pressing v.

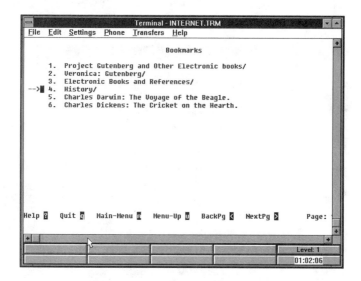

Figure 13.5 Viewing the bookmarks.

Trying to Find your way back to someplace you've been
before in Gopherspace can be very frustrating. If you think
you may ever need to return, create a bookmark, and enter
your own title if you wish—something you're more likely to
remember.

Using Veronica

Veronica is a system that helps you search through the
hundreds of servers in Gopherspace.

Veronica Veronica means *Very Easy Rodent-
Oriented Net-wide Index to Computerized
Archives.*

Most Gopher systems have a menu option for Veronica somewhere. Something like *Search Topics in Gopherspace Using Veronica/*. Select this option and you'll see something like Figure 13.6.

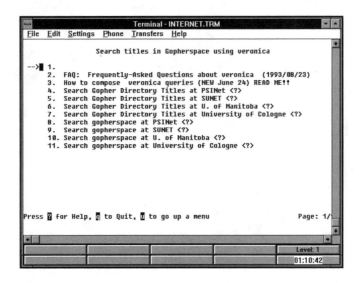

Figure 13.6 Veronica menu options.

There are different Veronica *servers*, computers containing Veronica databases. Your Gopher may show more than our illustration shows, or different ones.

There are two sorts of searches—you can search all titles, or just directory titles. The former searches for all information stored in Gopher servers—menu names (a menu is, in effect, the same as a directory), telnet connections, FTP connections, filenames, and so on. The directory-titles search only looks at the menus, not at the files.

A title search, therefore, results in a larger number of "hits" than a directory-titles search—perhaps many more. Where the directory-title list might be one page long, the titles search might be a dozen.

To search using Veronica, simply select a Search menu option, and type the word or words for which you want to search into the box, as in Figure 13.7.

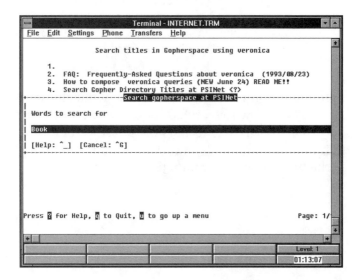

Figure 13.7 Searching with Veronica.

Press Enter to begin the search. In a few moments you'll see a new menu, containing what Veronica found for you. If one of the hits interests you, select it as you would any menu option and you'll be taken directly there.

Veronica is a fantastic tool for finding information in Gopherspace—in effect you are very quickly creating a menu of options in which you are interested, menu options that may be spread across several continents and dozens of countries.

You'll usually find plenty of entries that you don't want, though. For instance, when searching for Electronic Books, I found Phone and Address Books, E-mail Addresses and Telephone Books, and so on. You can quickly remove an entry by placing the arrow next to it and pressing d.

Create a Veronica Bookmark You can place the result of a Veronica search into your custom menu using the A command (to create a bookmark). Or select particular menu options, and use the a command. If you are using your service provider's Gopher, this will be saved when you close the client, and will be there the next time.

In this lesson you learned how to save documents and computer files, how to search Gopher menus, how to create your own Bookmark menu, and how to use Veronica to search *Gopherspace*. In the next lesson, you learn how to use telnetting to log into computers all over the world.

Lesson

Using Telnet

In this lesson you learn how to use telnet to work on computers all across the world.

Telnet is a special program that lets you "reach out" to computers all over the world and log onto them—you can use games and databases and programs on computers thousands of miles away. Telnet turns your computer into a telnet *client* to access data and programs on a telnet *server* somewhere. Because you are logging into a computer other than the one you connect to normally, "telnetting" is sometimes known as *remote login*.

There are two basic types of telnet access—private and public. Many Internet users have private telnet accounts—a researcher, for instance, may have several computers he or she works on regularly, and may have been given a special login name and password by the administrators of those computers.

Many computers also allow "strangers" into their systems. This is done on a purely voluntary basis, dependent on the goodwill of the people who own or operate a particular computer. If a telnet server is open to the public, anyone can get on the system and see what's available.

Telnet With Gopher You can use your Gopher to quickly and easily telnet to many telnet sites. See Lessons 12 and 13 for more information.

Starting Telnet

Telnetting, as it's known, is surprisingly easy. All you need to know is the host name of the computer that you want to reach, and perhaps a login name it will accept. Then you issue this command:

```
telnet hostname
```

You may need to specify a *port number* in addition to a host name. Simply leave a space, then type the number. For instance: telnet eve.assumption.edu 5000 takes you to a telnet site where you can play chess with other users. The 5000 is the port number.

When you connect to the computer, you may be prompted for a login name. You can enter the one you know is acceptable, or, if you don't have a login name, just type your own name. In some cases you won't even have to log in—the computer just lets you straight in without any kind of checks.

Trying HYTELNET

Perhaps the best way to try telnetting (and at the same time get an idea of what can be done by telnetting) is to use the HYTELNET system. Use this procedure:

1. Type telnet access.usask.ca and press Enter.

2. After a few moments you'll see this:

```
Trying 128.233.3.1 ...
Connected to access.usask.ca.
Escape character is '^]'.
ULTRIX V4.3 (Rev. 44) (access.usask.ca)
login:
```

3. Type hytelnet and press Enter. After a few moments you'll see the screen in Figure 14.1. You are now connected to a computer in Saskatchewan, Canada.

Figure 14.1   The HYTELNET main menu.

4. Notice the commands below the menu. You can use the up and down arrows to move the highlight up and down the menus; the right arrow (or Enter) to select a menu option; the left arrow to move to the previous menu; m to return to the main menu; and q—anywhere in the system—to end the session.

5. Press the down arrow until the highlight is on the Other Resources menu option. (There may be a delay in movement.)

> **Slow Responses?**   Telnet is very slow some-
> times. It can take several seconds, or even several
> minutes, for the telnet site to respond, depending
> on the amount of network traffic. If you find a task
> *too* slow, come back later.

6. Press Enter or the right arrow to select the option. You'll see Figure 14.2.

Figure 14.2 The Other Resources options.

7. Select the Databases and bibliographies option, and press Enter or the right arrow. You'll see a list of telnet sites. (See Figure 14.3.)

8. Press Spacebar to move through the list until you find an entry that interests you. (I'm going to use *<ful063> Music and Brain Information Database (MBI)* as an example.)

9. When you see an entry you want to know more about, press the down arrow key to move the highlight to the entry, and press Enter. You'll see information about the database. (See Figure 14.4.)

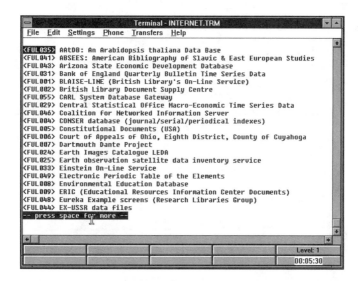

Figure 14.3 The Databases and Bibliographies entries.

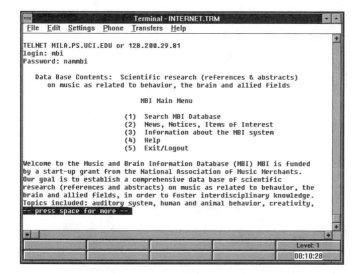

Figure 14.4 Information about the Music and Brain Information Database.

This information will usually show you the telnet host (for instance, in our example you would use the telnet mila.ps.uci.edu command to get to the Music and Brain Information Database), the login you need (mbi), and perhaps the password (nammbi). Sometimes the telnet site is private, but you may see an e-mail address or phone number for the person you must contact to gain access.

10. When you've finished reading, press left arrow to go back to the list.

11. Continue exploring in this way until you have finished with HYTELNET. Then, at any point in the menu structure, press q to end the session.

Play around in HYTELNET. You'll find descriptions of many resources—electronic books, NASA databases, library catalogs, the Biotechnet Electronic Buyers Guide, the Business Start-Up Information Database, and on and on—and which telnet site you need to go to if you want to use the resources.

Typing Disappears?   Can't see what you type when you are in a telnet session? See the **set echo** command later in this lesson.

All Systems Are Different

Once connected through telnet, what you see depends on what sort of system is set up on that computer. It might be a series of menus that let you select options, or it might be a prompt at which you type. You're simply logging onto a different computer, and each system varies a little.

In most cases you'll be presented with basic instructions on using the system. Spend some time reading this information. Some systems are well designed and easy to use. Others are poorly designed and very difficult to figure out.

About Your Terminal

Sometimes you'll be prompted to enter a terminal type before you start a telnet session. If you enter a terminal type that the other system doesn't recognize, you may not be able to see what's displayed on your screen. The most common terminal type, one that virtually all systems can use, is VT100. (Some communication programs have VT102 instead of VT100—they're pretty much the same.) Make sure you set your communications software to the same terminal type that you tell the telnet site to use.

Leaving a Telnet Site

Once you've logged on to a telnet site, you're in that computer's system, and each system is different. How do you leave the telnet site? Try q, quit, exit, Ctrl+d, or done, in that order. One of those will probably end the session and return you to the UNIX prompt. If none of these work, try Ctrl+] to return to a telnet> prompt, then type close and press Enter.

More Telnet Commands

You can start telnet and go to the telnet> prompt simply by typing telnet and pressing Enter. If you do this, you'll have to use the open command to start a session. You can't just type "telnet *hostname*" at the telnet> prompt—you'll have to use open *hostname* instead. Here are a few other commands you should know:

> **close**   Closes the connection to the telnet server. Use this if you get stuck somehow on the other computer and it doesn't let you log out—press Ctrl+] and then type close. If you issued the **telnet** command from the UNIX shell prompt, you'll go back there. If you used the **open** command, you'll go back to the telnet> prompt.

set echo   Telnet usually works with *remote echoing*. That means, when you type, the characters are sent to the server, which then sends them back—only then are they displayed on your screen. If they are *not* sent back—you notice that you don't see the command when you type it, but the command is still used by the telnet server—you can turn *local echoing* on with this command. Press Ctrl+] to get back to the telnet> prompt, then type set echo, press Enter, and press Enter again to return to the session. Repeat to turn local echoing off. Or use the set echo command if you see everything you type *twice*, to turn off local echo.

?   This command displays a list of telnet commands. But you can only issue it at the telnet> prompt—again, press Ctrl+] before typing ?.

In this lesson you learned how to use telnet to login to computers all over the world. In the next lesson, you learn how to transfer files from other computers back to your system.

Lesson

Using FTP

In this lesson you learn how to use FTP to transfer files from other computers.

There are millions of computer files available publicly on the Internet—public domain and shareware programs, books, pictures, sounds, just about anything. You can transfer these files back to your service provider's system using a program called *file transfer protocol*, or FTP for short. You'll often see the term *ftp* or *FTP*. In a directory or mail message you might be told to "ftp to such and such a computer to find this file." That simply means use the FTP system to grab the file.

FTP can be used for private transfers—in cases in which you have been given permission to get onto another computer and grab files—and in *anonymous* sessions. *Anonymous ftp* sessions are those in which you enter a system that's open to the public.

> **Searching for Files** You can use Archie to search all over the world for a computer file you are looking for. See Lesson 16.

A quick word about *when* to use FTP. Many systems don't like people digging around during business hours. They would rather you came in during evenings and weekends. So you may see a message asking you to restrict your use to after hours, or the FTP site may even not let you in at all during certain hours.

FTP Through Gopher

If you're lucky, your service provider has set up some kind of menu system to make FTP easy to use, possibly using a Gopher to help you find your way through the Internet to FTP sites. On my service provider's menu system, I can make this selection to see an FTP menu:

```
8. File Transfer (FTP)/
```

From there I can do various things, including connect to a specific FTP host and view FTP sites in alphabetical order by hostname/.

The first option expects me to enter the FTP site name. The second displays hundreds of different FTP sites in alphabetical order. Whichever way I use to get to one of the FTP sites, the system handles all the logging on for me, and displays file directories in the form of a menu. I can even download a file directly from FTP to my computer by using the **D** command.

This system makes running around an FTP site *much* easier than using FTP itself (as you'll soon realize as you read on). For more information on Gopher, see Lessons 12 and 13.

FTP to Project Gutenberg

As an example, let's FTP to Project Gutenberg, a project in which important books, speeches, articles, and so on are being converted to electronic format. Follow this procedure:

1. At the UNIX shell, type ftp mrcnext.cso.uiuc.edu and press Enter. You'll see something like this:

```
Connected to mrcnext.cso.uiuc.edu.
220 mrcnext.cso.uiuc.edu FTP server (Version
5.1 (NeXT 1.0) Tue Jul 21, 1992) ready.
Name (mrcnext.cso.uiuc.edu:peterk):
```

Can't Connect?   Your system may not connect, depending on how busy the Project Gutenberg site is. Try again later.

2. Type anonymous and press Enter. You'll see this:

```
331 Guest login ok, send ident as pass-
word.
Password:
```

3. Type your e-mail address and press Enter (you won't see it as you type). You'll then see an introductory message, followed by the **ftp>** prompt. The introductory message currently states that the Project Gutenberg files are in the **/pub/etext** directory.

Login Mistakes   If you make a mistake while logging in, the login will fail. Type user anonymous (or substitute the login name you've been assigned for anonymous), and press Enter. (This won't always work, because the remote system may close the connection.)

4. Type pwd and press Enter to see what directory you are in right now. (You are probably in the / directory, the root directory.)

5. To move to the **etext** directory, type cd /pub/etext and press Enter.

6. Type dir and press Enter to see what's in this directory.

Reading Directories   Long directories are difficult to read in FTP. See the FTP commands in the Appendix. Or use your communications program to copy all the incoming data to a text file. And check to see if your communications program lets you scroll back to see earlier in the session—if so, you can scroll back up to view the top of the directory listing.

7. Some of the files are text files containing information about what files are available. Type get INDEX100.GUT "|more" and press Enter to see the file in Figure 15.1.

Looking for Index Files   FTP sessions are not usually this easy, because you don't know which file contains the information you want. You often have to try several before you find the right one.

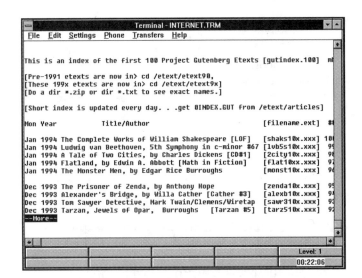

Figure 15.1   The INDEX100.GUT text file.

8. Read through this text file until you find a text
you'd like to copy. Make a note of the filename (for
example, **zenda10x.xxx**). Notice also the date of
the file. At the top of the text file it says that pre-
1991 files are in a directory called **/pub/etext/
etext90**, while later texts are in a directory dependent on the year—1993 texts are in **/pub/etext/
etext93**, for instance.

Press Spacebar to move down a page, Ctrl+c to end
viewing the file.

9. At the ftp> prompt, type dir and press Enter. You'll
notice that there are some directories called
etext9x, where **x** is the last digit of the year. (Directories are indicated by the **d** at the beginning of the
line.)

10. Type cd etext9*x* and press Enter. For instance, if the
date of the text you want is 1993, type cd etext93
and press Enter.

11. Now type dir followed by the first few characters of
the filename you want, followed by an asterisk. For
instance, for zenda10x.xxx type dir zen*. Press
Enter, and you'll see a list of matches. If you are in
etext93 and tried dir zen*, you see this:

```
      ftp> dir zen*
      200 PORT command successful.
      150 Opening ASCII mode data connection
      for /bin/ls.
      -rw-r—r—  1 hart      wheel      308591
Dec 10 22:15 zenda10.txt
      -rw-r—r—  1 hart      wheel      130194
Dec 10 22:15 zenda10.zip
      226 Transfer complete.
      remote: zen*
      132 bytes received in 0.0018 seconds
      (71 Kbytes/s)
```

12. There are two matching files: one is a .txt file (an ASCII text file), the other a .zip file (a PKZip compressed file for the PC—to decompress it you need the PKUnzip utility). The .zip file is much smaller than the .txt file, as you can see from the file size preceding the date.

13. If you want a text file, you must do an ASCII transfer—type ascii and press Enter. If you want a zip file, you must do a binary transfer—type binary and press Enter.

> **System Crashes?**   If you send a non-text file by an ASCII transfer, FTP—or even your computer itself—might lock up. Sending an ASCII text file as binary takes a little longer than necessary, but doesn't do any harm.

14. Now type get followed by the filename you want—for instance: get zenda10.txt. Press Enter and the file is transferred to your service provider's computer.

> **Is Anything Happening?**   Before transferring a large file, use the hash command—FTP displays hash marks (#) to show that it's actually doing something during transmission (so you don't think it's locked up).

15. Type close and press Enter. This takes you back to the UNIX prompt. You can also try the quit or bye commands. Or press Ctrl+d.

There are a lot of FTP commands available, and a lot of ways to run into problems in FTP. For more information, see the FTP commands in the Appendix.

In this lesson you learned how to use FTP to transfer files from computers all over the world. In the next lesson, you learn how to use Archie to track down files you may need.

Lesson

16

Using Archie to Find Files

In this lesson you learn how to use Archie to track down computer files anywhere on the Internet.

How do you know where to go to find the file you want? Sometimes you'll see the FTP site mentioned in e-mail or a document you found somewhere. But if you know the file you are looking for—but have no idea where to find it—you can use Archie to help you. Archie indexes FTP sites, listing the files that are available at each site—several million files at over a thousand FTP sites.

Getting to Archie

You can use Archie in a couple of ways. You may use an Archie *client* on your service provider's computer, either from a menu option or a shell command. Or you can telnet to an Archie *server* site.

If your service provider's system has an Archie client setup, you should use it instead of telnetting to an Archie server, because it will cut down on network traffic. However, it has limitations—it may be much slower than telnetting to a server, and you won't be able to do everything that you could do if you telnetted. We'll take a look at telnet first.

Using Telnet

There are Archie servers all over the world—here are a few in the U.S.:

Address	Location
archie.ans.net	USA, ANS
archie.internic.net	USA, AT&T (NY)
archie.rutgers.edu	USA, Rutgers Univ.
nic.sura.net	USA, SURAnet
archie.unl.edu	USA, Univ. of Nebraska

List of Archies   To find the latest list of Archie servers, send an e-mail message to an Archie server—**archie@archieserver** (for example, archie@archie.rutgers.edu). In the body of the message, type servers on the first line.

If you can, use the Archie closest to you. That generates less network traffic. But some servers may be too busy to get onto, and some systems have a policy of denying *everyone* access between certain hours (8:00 a.m. and 8:00 p.m., for instance). You can use the server later, or try another.

Starting the Session

How, then, to telnet to Archie? At the UNIX shell, (for instance), type telnet archie.rutgers.edu. When asked to log in, simply type archie and press Enter.

First One is Busy   If the first Archie site is busy, try another—you may find yourself at the telnet> prompt, so don't use the telnet command. Instead, type open *archieserver* (for instance, open archie.rutgers.edu) and press Enter.

Selecting a Search Type

Before you begin searching for a filename, you ought to figure out the *type* of search that you want to use:

exact   You must type the exact name of the file for which you are looking.

regex   You will type a UNIX *regular expression*. That means that Archie will regard some of the characters in the word you type as *wildcards*. If you don't understand regular expressions, don't use this type of search.

sub   Archie will search *within* filenames for what you type. That is, it will look for all names that are the same, or that *include* the characters you typed. For instance, if you are searching for **textwin**, it will find "textwin" *and* "textwindows." And you don't need to worry about the case of the characters—Archie will find "textwindows" *and* "TextWindows."

subcase   This is like the **sub** search, except you need to get the case of the word correct—if you ask for "textwin," Archie will find "textwindows," but not "TextWindows."

> **Use Sub**   You'll probably want to use the **sub** search. It takes a little longer, but it's much easier to use than the other types.

To make sure the server you're working with is using the type of search you want, type set search *type* (for instance, set search sub) and press Enter.

Searching for a File

Use the **prog** command to search for the file you want. Let's search for **textwin**. First, we're going to set the search type to **sub**. Then we'll search.

```
archie> set search sub
archie> prog textwin
```

When Archie begins, you may see something like this:

```
# Search type: sub.
# Your queue position: 3
# Estimated time for completion: 00:19
working... ¦
```

Or you may see a line that shows the percentage of the database searched. Or you may see nothing at all (which is frustrating, because it can take several minutes for Archie to search the database).

If you are lucky—and Archie finds something—you'll eventually see something like this:

```
Location: /contrib/src/pa/ups-2.45/mips-
ultrix/ups
FILE       rwxr-xr-x        23   Oct 28 06:43
textwin.c -> ../../src/ups/textwin.c
FILE       rwxr-xr-x        23   Oct 28 06:43
textwin.h -> ../../src/ups/textwin.
Location: /contrib/src/pa/ups-2.45/src/ups
FILE       r--r--r--     18985   May 20  1992
textwin.c
FILE       r--r--r--      2542   May  3  1991
textwin.h


Host csn.org    (128.138.213.21)
Last updated 19:45  4 May 1993
Location: /pub/dos
DIRECTORY rwxrwxr-x       512   Mar 29 04:01
textwin
```

```
Host faui43.informatik.uni-erlangen.de
(131.188.1.43)
Last updated 08:17  7 May 1993
Location: /mounts/epix/iwiftp/public/portal/
amiga/amok/amok58
FILE       rw-r--r--      10132  Feb 15 20:29
TextWindows.lzh
Location: /mounts/epix/iwiftp/public/portal/
amiga/amok/amok68
FILE       rw-r--r--      10928  Feb 15 20:30
TextWindows_1.1.lha
```

Long Archie Lists   If the list is long, and shoots by before you can read it, use the set pager command, then do the search again. Now the list stops after each page, and you can press Spacebar to see the next page, or q and Enter to stop the listing. Turn off this feature using unset pager.

In this example, we found a program called **TextWindows** and one called **textwin**. Notice the words **FILE** and **DIRECTORY** on the left side of the listing—Archie searches for both files and directories that match your criteria.

Above each listing there's a **Location**, showing the directory in which you should look for this file or subdirectory. A line or two above the Location, you'll see the **Host** line: this is the host computer to which you should "ftp" to get the file (see Lesson 15). For instance, if you wanted to get the last file in our list, you would ftp to **faui43.informatik.uni-erlangen.de** (a computer somewhere in Germany), and go into the following directory:

/mounts/epix/iwiftp/public/portal/amiga/amok/amok68

Mail It Home

If you are doing a lot of Archie searches, or get a very long list, you can send the information home to your e-mail address. Type mail *emailaddress* and press Enter. The last list that Archie found for you is sent to your e-mail inbox. If you plan to use this feature several times, you can even store your e-mail address (temporarily). First, type set mailto *emailaddress* and press Enter. Now you can type the mail command alone, without bothering to include the e-mail address.

Using the Whatis Search

Archie has *descriptive index* that you can search. Not all files indexed by Archie have a description, but many do. For instance, you might type:

```
archie> whatis space
```

You would see a long listing of descriptions, including these:

```
ds              Disk Space Available
dusage          Filter the output of du(1) and
                produce a report about
newspace        Determine newsgroup disk usage
noback          Convert lines with backspaces
                in them to multiple line
nobs            Backspace filter
tab             Indent a file one tab, or a
                specified number of spaces
tabs            A tab/space conversion program
xinvaders       Space invaders for X11
```

You may not be able to figure out how your keyword fits with some of these files, but no matter, as long as some of them look like what you want. Notice the word on the left side of each line. If you want to find out where the listed file is, type prog *name*. For instance, **prog xinvaders** would list the X11 "Space invaders" files.

Closing Archie

When you have finished working in Archie, type exit and press Enter. You'll return to the UNIX shell or ftp> prompt.

Using Your Service Provider's Client

Many service providers have loaded Archie clients. That means you don't have to worry about finding a client or a server—you can just select Archie from a menu or use a UNIX command to use it.

> **Slow Service**   Using Archie from your service provider's system can prove *very* slow, so slow you might think it's locked up. If you get tired of waiting, Ctrl+c should stop it.

Using your service provider's client is different from using the Archie server itself. You won't use the **prog** command, and you won't set the type of search *before* searching—you'll specify it at the same time. Here's how you can enter a command at the UNIX prompt:

```
archie searchtype searchterm
```

For instance, this command would do a *sub* search for **textwin**:

```
teal% archie -s textwin
```

This command would tell the provider's client to look for any filename that contains the letters **textwin**, and it wouldn't care about case—it would find TextWindows or textwin. These are the *searchtypes*:

-e   Archie will do an *exact* search.

-r   Archie will do a *regex* search.

-s   Archie will do a *sub* search.

-c   Archie will do a *subc* search.

Saving It in a File

If you wish, you can copy the results into a file by following the name you are searching for with >*textfilename*. For instance:

```
archie -s textwin >textw.txt
```

This command will do a *sub* search for the name **textwin**, and copy the output into a file called **textw.txt**. This is useful when you are likely to get a big list, or if you want to save the information and use it later.

Archie by Mail

You can also use Archie by e-mail. You can avoid hanging around waiting for Archie to search, and you can reduce network traffic.

Send a message to **mail archie@*archieaddress*** (for instance, mail archie@archie.rutgers.edu). **Put the commands in the body of the message. The commands are mostly the same as the ones you use when telnetting to an Archie site, but send the command help to get the Archie site to send you a mail-user guide.

In this lesson you learned how to use Archie to track down files you may need. In the next lesson, you learn how to transfer files from your service provider's computer back to your own computer.

17

Transferring Files to Your Computer

In this lesson you learn how to transfer files from your service provider's computer back to your computer.

If you have a dial-in terminal account, you are working at home or in your office on your computer, which is connected to your service provider's computer. When you *get* files using FTP, where do they go? Back to your directory on the service provider's computer. Now you have to get them back to your computer.

There are several ways to do this. Most communication programs let you do an *xmodem* transfer, so we'll look at that first.

Xmodem

Most communications programs can work with xmodem to transmit files. It's quite easy. First, make sure your communication program is set up to receive files by xmodem. For instance, if you are using Windows Terminal, select Binary Transfers from the Settings menu, then click on the Xmodem option button.

Now, at the UNIX shell, type the xmodem command, starting with xmodem, and followed by one of these:

sb   Send binary—use this if you are sending a binary file—any computer file other than an ASCII text file.

st   Send text—use this if you are sending a text
(ASCII) file to an MS-DOS computer.

sa   Send Apple—use this if you are sending a text
(ASCII) file to an Apple computer.

> **Sending Files**   If you are going the other
> way—sending files from *your* computer to the
> service provider's computer—use the rb, rt, and
> ra commands (Receive Binary, Receive Text, and
> Receive Apple).

Then follow these by the filename. So, for instance,

```
xmodem st zap.txt
```

sends the file named **zap.txt** in ASCII format. After typing
the command and pressing Enter, you see this:

```
XMODEM Version 3.9 (November 1990) — UNIX-
Microcomputer File Transfer Facility
File zap.txt Ready to SEND in text mode
Estimated File Size 2K, 15 Sectors, 1845
Bytes
Estimated transmission time 2 seconds
Send several Control-X characters to cancel
```

You then tell your communications program to receive
the file—in Windows Terminal, you select Receive Binary
File from the Transfers menu (even if you are transmitting a
text file, you are using a binary-transfer method to transmit
it). You have to tell your communications program what
filename to use. When the transfer is complete, you are
returned to the UNIX shell prompt.

Overwriting Files   Be careful when transferring files. These systems usually overwrite files that have the same names as the ones being transferred. If you use zmodem you can use the **-p** switch (as in sz -p *filename*) to make sure files aren't overwritten, but test it before you trust it.

Zmodem

The xmodem protocol is not necessarily your best option. Zmodem, for instance, is much better. It's much faster, and while xmodem can send multiple files with a bit of messing around (assuming your communications software can *accept* multiple files, which it may not be able to do), zmodem makes it easy to send several files at once.

To run zmodem, begin by setting up your communications program to receive zmodem transfers (Windows Terminal can't use zmodem, though many other programs can). Then at the UNIX shell, use this command:

```
sz filename
```

You can actually send several files at a time. For instance, sz *.txt sends all the .txt files in the directory, sz file1 file2 sends both file1 and file2.

Command Summary   To see a summary of all the options, type sz and press Enter at the prompt.

Once you issue the command, that's it—you don't have to tell your system anything about the incoming files—as long as you've got **zmodem receive** set up, your communications program automatically detects when the service provider's computer is sending data, and even figures out the filenames.

Sending Files When transferring files from your computer to the service providers, zmodem is also very simple: you begin the transfer from your communications program; the service provider's computer detects it, and begins receiving automatically.

There are a few command *switches* you need to know about when using zmodem:

-b   Sends the file in binary format. This is the default anyway, so you won't normally need to use this.

-a   This, in effect, sends an ASCII file to a DOS machine—it converts the UNIX new line character at the end of each line to the DOS carriage return/line feed characters.

-p   This tells your computer not to overwrite any existing files with the same name. But this option doesn't always work; experiment with it before you rely on it.

You can combine these. For instance, sz -ap *filename* sends a text file and ensures that it doesn't overwrite a file of the same name.

More Information If you want more information about zmodem or xmodem, use the man sz or man xmodem command to see the online manual.

In this lesson you learned how to transfer data from your service provider's computer back to your own. In the next lesson, you learn how to use a Wide Area Information Server to search hundreds of Internet databases throughout the world.

Lesson

Using WAIS

18

In this lesson you learn how to use a WAIS, a Wide Area Information Server, to search hundreds of databases at once.

WAIS, the *Wide Area Information Server*, is a system that helps you search for documents containing information you want. WAIS provides an index of over 600 databases, lets you select the ones you want to search, and carries out a search for you. If it finds what you want, it can then save the documents, sending them to you via e-mail or in a file.

The databases contain tens of thousands of documents, from the archives of various newsgroups to weather reports, zip codes, articles about computer archaeology, and reviews of kids' software. Most of the files contain text documents, though you can also find sounds, graphics, and so on.

Getting Started

As with Gopher, there are several ways to run WAIS:

- Telnet to quake.think.com or nnsc.nsf.net and run WAIS from there.
- Run WAIS on your service provider's system from a menu option.
- Run WAIS on your service provider's system from the UNIX shell.
- Run WAIS from a Gopher menu option.

As usual, there are different types of WAIS interfaces available. The one you can get to by telnetting is *swais*, a UNIX-based, character-oriented WAIS server. There are WAIS systems available for just about any computer system available—DOS, Windows, Macintosh, X Windows, NeXT, and so on. They all work differently, and some have more features than others. We're going to look at the swais version, probably the simplest one. Ask your service provider what you have available.

Telnetting to WAIS

Let's take a look at WAIS. You're going to use telnet to get to a WAIS server. You can telnet to quake.think.com, or nnsc.nsf.net and log in as wais.

```
teal% telnet quake.think.com
Trying 192.31.181.1 ...
Connected to quake.think.com.
Escape character is '^]'.
SunOS UNIX (quake)

login: wais
Last login: Fri Mar 25 17:44:19 from
nyplgate.nypl.or
SunOS Release 4.1.3 (SUN4C-STANDARD) #9: Wed
Oct 27 18:18:30 EDT 1993
Welcome to swais.
Please type user identifier (optional, i.e
user@host): peterk@csn.org
TERM = (vt100) (press Enter)
```

You should see a message explaining that WAIS has changed, and you are about to see the *directory of servers*. When you have finished reading the message (when you press q), you'll see Figure 18.1, the Source Selection screen. Previous versions of WAIS used to show you a list of all the WAIS databases, and you would pick the ones you wanted to search. Now, though, the system shows a single entry, the

directory of servers, and lets you search it for the names of
servers that may have information you want.

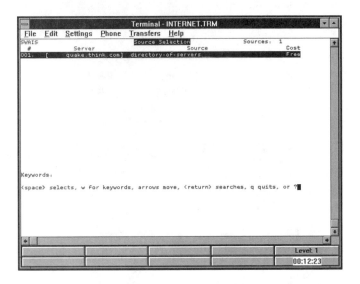

Figure 18.1   The WAIS Source Selection screen.

Press Enter to search the directory of servers—the
Keywords: line at the bottom is highlighted. Remember,
right now you are going to search *for* a database, not *within*
a database, so don't use a keyword that is too specific. Type
a keyword, and press Enter to begin the search. After a few
seconds WAIS displays the result. If you search for **education**, for instance, you would see something like Figure 18.2.

To find information about any of these, select the entry
and press Enter. You'll see information about where the
database is stored, who to contact for more information, and
what the database contains.

If you decide that one of the entries in this new list
might be useful, highlight it in the list and press u. WAIS
adds it to the Source Selection list.

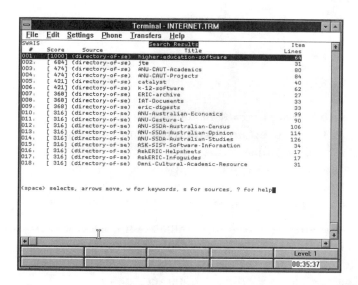

Figure 18.2 The result from the **education** search.

Moving Around in a List

Use these commands while working in a list of databases:

Move the cursor down one entry	j or down arrow or Ctrl+n
Move the cursor down one screen	J or Ctrl+v or Ctrl+d
Move the cursor up one entry	k or up arrow or Ctrl+p
Move the cursor up one screen	K or Ctrl+u
Move to a particular line	type the number and press Enter
Read about the highlighted database	Enter (type q and Enter to return to the listing)
Return to the Source Selection list	s

| View the Help screen | h or ? |
| Quit | q |

WAIS Found Nothing

If WAIS doesn't find any matches, it displays a line that says **Search produced no result**. Press Enter and you'll see a catalog of the available databases. (Each **Document** in this list is a database.) You can page through this list to find something that looks useful, note the **Headline:** entry, then return to the Search Results screen by pressing q.

Then press s to return to the Source Selection screen, and use the **Headline:** entry as the keyword—WAIS finds the database for you, and you can then use u to move the database to the Source Selection screen.

Searching a Database

When you've selected the databases you want to search (and moved them to the Source Selection screen using the u command), press s to return to the Source Selection screen.

Now select the databases you are going to search. Highlight each one and press Spacebar. You can use the keystrokes we looked at earlier to move around in the Source Selection screen, as well as these:

Select an entry (or deselect a selected entry)	Spacebar or .(period)
Deselect all selections	=
Select an entry and move to keywords field	Ctrl+j
Search selected entries with keywords	Enter
Enter keywords on which to search	w and then press Enter. (Press Ctrl+C to cancel)

Move the cursor through the list, and press Spacebar or (period) to select the entries you want to search—you can select as many as you want. Then press w. You can now type a new keyword into the **Keyword:** line at the bottom of the screen.

What sort of keywords can you use? You can enter several words, separated by spaces. You can only do a simple keyword search, though—WAIS will search for each word you enter, so you can't do a *Boolean* search (MATH AND SPELL, for instance).

> **Boolean Searches**   Searches in which you specify multiple search criteria, limiting them with AND, IF, and OR statements.

Keywords must start with a letter, not a number. And you may only use one type of punctuation character inside words—a period, for instance, as in "I.B.M."

> **Missing Keyword?**   When you press Enter to begin a search, you may notice the **Keywords:** field is empty, though the text cursor is not at the left side—it's indented a little. Your keyword is still there, you just can't see it. Press Enter to continue. Or delete it by using your Delete or Backspace key (or try Ctrl+H or # if they don't work) and type another one.

For instance, I selected the **k-12-software**. Then I entered these keywords:

```
Keywords: math spelling
```

After a few moments I saw the screen in Figure 18.3.

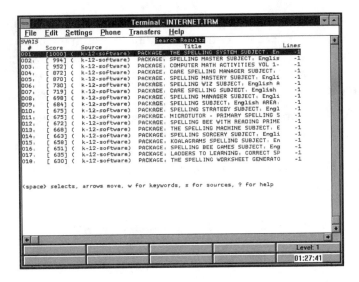

```
┌────────────────────────────────────────────────────────────────┐
│ ▬             Terminal - INTERNET.TRM                    ▼ ▲    │
│ File  Edit  Settings  Phone  Transfers  Help                   │
│ SWAIS                              Search Results              ↑ │
│  #    Score    Source               Title              Lines   │
│ 001:  [1000] ( k-12-software)  PACKAGE: THE SPELLING SYSTEM SUBJECT: En  -1 │
│ 002:  [ 994] ( k-12-software)  PACKAGE: SPELLING MASTER SUBJECT: Englis  -1 │
│ 003:  [ 952] ( k-12-software)  PACKAGE: COMPUTER MATH ACTIVITIES VOL 1-  -1 │
│ 004:  [ 872] ( k-12-software)  PACKAGE: CARE SPELLING MANAGER SUBJECT:   -1 │
│ 005:  [ 870] ( k-12-software)  PACKAGE: SPELLING MASTERY SUBJECT: Engli  -1 │
│ 006:  [ 730] ( k-12-software)  PACKAGE: SPELLING WIZ SUBJECT: English A  -1 │
│ 007:  [ 719] ( k-12-software)  PACKAGE: CARE SPELLING SUBJECT: English   -1 │
│ 008:  [ 698] ( k-12-software)  PACKAGE: SPELLING MANAGER SUBJECT: Engli  -1 │
│ 009:  [ 684] ( k-12-software)  PACKAGE: SPELLING SUBJECT: English AREA:  -1 │
│ 010:  [ 675] ( k-12-software)  PACKAGE: SPELLING STRATEGY SUBJECT: Engl  -1 │
│ 011:  [ 675] ( k-12-software)  PACKAGE: MICROTUTOR - PRIMARY SPELLING S  -1 │
│ 012:  [ 672] ( k-12-software)  PACKAGE: SPELLING BEE WITH READING PRIME  -1 │
│ 013:  [ 668] ( k-12-software)  PACKAGE: THE SPELLING MACHINE SUBJECT: E  -1 │
│ 014:  [ 663] ( k-12-software)  PACKAGE: SPELLING SORCERY SUBJECT: Engli  -1 │
│ 015:  [ 658] ( k-12-software)  PACKAGE: KOALAGRAMS SPELLING SUBJECT: En  -1 │
│ 016:  [ 651] ( k-12-software)  PACKAGE: SPELLING BEE GAMES SUBJECT: Eng  -1 │
│ 017:  [ 635] ( k-12-software)  PACKAGE: LADDERS TO LEARNING: CORRECT SP  -1 │
│ 018:  [ 630] ( k-12-software)  PACKAGE: THE SPELLING WORKSHEET GENERATO  -1 │
│                                                                │
│ <space> selects, arrows move, w for keywords, s for sources, ? for help │
│                                                                │
│                                                                │
│                                                                │
│ ←                                                          →   │
│                                                   Level: 1     │
│                                                   01:27:41     │
└────────────────────────────────────────────────────────────────┘
```

Figure 18.3 The result from the **math spelling** search.

Returning to Database List To get back to the list of databases, press s.

Reading and Saving the Information

You can now move through this list, in the same way you moved through the database list. This list, however, is of documents, not databases. When you press Spacebar or Enter, you can read the highlighted document.

Jumbled Lines? Sometimes documents are displayed slightly jumbled up, so the lines are not consecutive. If that happens, try this: Go to the list and highlight the document you want to read. Then press l, type more, and press Enter.

You can send the document to yourself—or anyone else, for that matter—using e-mail. Press m. You'll be prompted for an e-mail address. Type the address, press Enter, and it's on its way. If the WAIS client program is on your service provider's computer, you can use the S command to save the document in a file.

In this lesson you learned how to use WAIS to search many of the Internet's databases. In the next lesson, you learn how to use the Internet's hypertext system, the World Wide Web.

Lesson

Using World Wide Web

In this lesson you learn how to use World Wide Web, the Internet's hypertext system.

The World Wide Web (*WWW, The Web,* or sometimes even *W3*) is a hypertext system that helps you travel around the world looking for information. Rather than searching for a keyword (as you do with WAIS), with WWW you follow a "trail" of linked words. You select a topic that interests you, and view related information—from which you select another topic that interests you, and see information related to that topic. In this way you move from one topic to another, moving closer to where you want to be. WWW is very easy to use, probably the easiest Internet tool you'll find.

> **Hypertext** A hypertext document is one that lets you jump from place to place in the document using links of some kind. Rather than reading the document from front to back, you can select a piece of text and move to a piece of related text elsewhere in the document.

Getting to the Web

There are several ways to use the Web:

- You can telnet to a WWW browser.

- There may be a menu option in your service provider's menu system. This may be a shortcut that uses telnet to get you to a WWW browser, or your service provider may have installed a WWW browser on the system.

- From the UNIX shell you can use a command that your service provider has set up to automatically connect to a WWW browser.

Browser   A program that knows how to search through the hypertext files of the World Wide Web.

Whichever method you use, you will be using a browser. Some, such as Mosaic, are quite fancy, appearing more like Windows Help systems, with underlined text (instead of bracketed numbers) to denote topics you can select. You're going to look at the simplest browser, however, because it's probably the one you'll be using: a text-based system (or *line-mode browser*).

Telnetting to the WWW

As an example of using the World Wide Web, we're going to use the browser at **info.cern.ch** at the European Particle Physics Laboratory in Switzerland. (We're going to use telnet to get us there.) You may also check with your service provider to see how else you can get to a WWW browser.

At the UNIX shell, type telnet info.cern.ch or telnet nxoc01.cern.ch and press Enter. When you connect, you'll see the top of the World Wide Web (see Figure 19.1).

Can't Connect?   If the system can't connect, there may be too many people using the system already. Try again later.

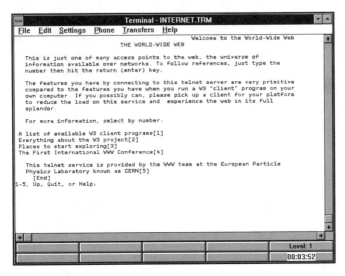

Figure 19.1 The "Welcome" screen.

Notice that we didn't have to log in—when you telnet to this location, you are placed into WWW automatically.

Using WWW

Once you are connected to the World Wide Web, you'll notice that there are numbers in brackets scattered throughout the system. Each bracketed number represents a hypertext link. Press the number and then press Enter, and you see another screen with related information.

For instance, a good place to start in our example (see Figure 19.1) would be with the topic called **Places to start exploring [3]**. (You may see something different from what's shown in this example.) Press 1 and Enter, and you see something like Figure 19.2.

You could then type 2 and press Enter to select **by Subject [1]**. This takes us to a subject list.

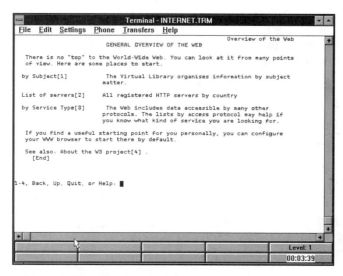

Figure 19.2 The General Overview screen.

The WWW Commands

Here are the commands you use when moving through the
WWW. Type each command and then press Enter.

These help you move through the current document:

Go down one page	Press Enter
Go to the previous page	u or up
Go to the last page	bo or bottom
Go to the first page	t or top
Search a document for a keyword	f keywords or find keywords (only when you see FIND on the prompt line).

These help you move between documents:

Go to a [number] reference press	Type the number and Enter.

See a list of [ ] references	l or list
Go to the previous document	b or back
Go to the first document you saw	ho or home
List the documents you've seen	r or recall
Go to a document in the Recall list	r number or recall number
View the next reference from the last document	n or next

These are general-purpose commands:

Display the Help page	h or help
Display the WWW manual	m or manual
Quit	quit

In particular, remember the ho or home command to take you back to the top of the system, and the r or recall command to see a list of where you've been. (To go to one of the documents in the recall list, type r *number* and press Enter.)

Home Doesn't Work? Sometimes the **ho** or **home** command won't work. Try using the b or back command instead, or the r or recall command.

WWW Stuck? WWW gets "stuck" sometimes, also. You'll find that some of the topic numbers don't work. Just back up and try again.

Play with these commands while you're working in WWW, and you'll soon get the hang of it. Just type the topic number and press Enter to select a particular topic. Then move down the topic, whether it's a listing or document, by pressing Enter. Move back up a page by pressing u and then Enter. To go back to where you just came from, use b and Enter. Take a look at the command table in this lesson, and try navigating through the web.

Exploring WWW

By selecting Places to start exploring [3], followed by the by Subject [1] topic, we can reach a subject listing (as shown in Figure 19.3), the "virtual library."

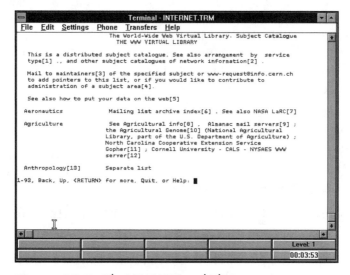

Figure 19.3 The WWW Virtual Library.

Press Enter to move through this list until you find an interesting subject. Then type the number and press Enter. You'll notice that some subjects have several topic numbers, others have just one and then the words "Separate list." This means that selecting that topic leads to another list of topics.

For instance, if you select **Electronic Journals[30]** (by typing 30 and pressing Enter), you'll see a list of electronic journals and print periodicals that have been put online. Select, for example, **Mother Jones[18]** and you'll see a variety of topics. Select **March/April[8]** under the **1994** heading to see a list of articles from that issue of the magazine. You could select **KAFKA'S BANKER[2]** to read an article about a banker who was lured into working for the CIA, for instance.

Saving the Information

The Web is not always very helpful when you want to save something. If you are using a WWW browser set up by your service provider, you can use the print command to print a document, or the > *filename* command (on a UNIX system) to save the document in a file (use >> *filename* to append it to the end of an existing file). Unfortunately, WWW doesn't currently provide a way to mail documents back to you the way, for instance, WAIS can do.

Using Gopher et al

You'll sometimes find yourself using other "resources" from the WWW. You may select a topic and notice something like this, for instance:

```
gopher://orion.lib.virginia.edu:70/11/alpha/bmcr
```

WWW has just hooked into Gopher, and taken you to a computer connected through the Gopher menu system. Or you may see this:

```
Connection Machine WAIS server.
```

WWW has connected through the WAIS system.

You can connect through WWW to WAIS, Gopher, FTP, and various other Internet systems. And you can use Telnet from your own WWW browser (though not from a public one like nxoc01.cern.ch). But WWW probably won't always work well for you in these other systems.

You may be able to view a document through WAIS and Gopher, but you won't be able to download a file. And if you try to view a binary file through FTP, for instance, WWW may try to do it, but at best you'll see garbage on your screen—at worst it will crash your computer. Still, you can use WWW to find what you are looking for—it can be easier to use WWW to search directories on a distant computer, for instance, than FTP. Then you can use FTP to go back to that system to grab the files you need.

In this lesson you learned how to work with the World Wide Web. In the next lesson, you learn how to track down interesting things to see and do on the Internet.

Lesson

Finding Things to Do on the Internet

*In this lesson you learn how to quickly track down infor-
mation about things to do and places to go on the Internet.*

It's all well and good knowing how to get around the
Internet, but where do you *go*? This lesson explains how to
find certain text files that will help you hunt down useful
and entertaining Internet sites.

Newsgroup Listings

David Lawrence publishes four files with lists of thousands of
newsgroups—two that list the USENET newsgroups, and two
listing "alternative" or non-USENET newsgroups. You can
find these in the news.announce.newusers newsgroup.

LISTSERV Listing

You can obtain a list of over 4,000 LISTSERV discussion
groups, with a short description of each one, by sending an
e-mail message to listserv@bitnic.educom.edu. In the body of
the message, type list global.

More Mailing Lists

Stephanie da Silva publishes a file containing almost 700
mailing-list discussion groups. You've seen (in Lesson 11)
how LISTSERV mailing lists work as discussion groups, and a

number of the mailing lists in this document are LISTSERV groups. This file also contains many more that are not LISTSERV groups, but work in the same way.

You can find this list by ftping to pit-manager.mit.edu, and changing to the pub/usenet/news.announce.newusers directory. The information is stored in several files currently called Publicly_Accessible_Mailing_Lists,_Part_*n*_6.

Finding Mailing Lists

Arno Wouters publishes *How to Find an Interesting Mailinglist*. You can get a copy of this file by sending e-mail to LISTSERV@vm1.nodak.edu with the command GET NEW-LIST WOUTERS in the body of the message. Or FTP to vm1.nodak.edu, change to the new-list directory, and get the new-list.wouters file.

BIGFUN.TXT

BIGFUN.TXT, compiled by Jeremy Smith, is a compilation of stuff that you can find on the Internet—Coke machines and fortune cookies, U.S. Geological Survey Maps, Harris Polls, information on solar flares, the exact time, book reviews—almost 20 pages of it.

You can find this file by ftping to ftp.csos.orst.edu. Log in as anonymous, change to the /pub/networking/bigfun directory, and get bigfun.txt.

Special Internet Connections

Scott Yanoff's *Special Internet Connections* file (sometimes known as the *Internet Services file*) contains all sorts of goodies, from archaeological databases to White House press releases.

You can find this file in a variety of places. It's published in the **alt.internet.services** newsgroup, you can get it by ftping or Gophering to csd4.csd.uwm.edu (get /pub/

inet.services.txt), and you can send an e-mail message to bbslist@aug3.augsburg.edu (the recipient *autoreplies* by sending the list to you automatically).

Internetwork Mail Guide

If you run into problems sending e-mail to particular Internet users, get hold of the *Internetwork Mail Guide*, created by Scott Yanoff. You can find the latest version of the file via anonymous ftp, at csd4.csd.uwm.edu (change to the pub directory, then get the file named internetwork-mail-guide).

Computer Science FTP Sites

Mac Su-Cheong publishes a small file that lists FTP sites containing information related to computer science. You can get the latest version of the list using the **finger** command: at the UNIX prompt, type finger msc@eembox.ncku.edu.tw >ftp-comp.txt to copy the list into a text file called **ftp-comp.txt**.

Libraries

Billy Barron and Marie-Christine Mahe publish *Accessing On-Line Bibliographic Databases*, a report with lots of information about libraries, throughout the Americas, Europe, Africa, and Asia.

You can find a copy of these files by anonymous ftp at ftp.utdallas.edu. Change to the /pub/staff/billy/libgui directory and get the libraries files. You can also Gopher to yaleinfo.yale.edu 7000, and select the Libraries directory. (Or select Yale University from a gopher directory, then select / Research and library services/More research & library services at Yale and beyond/Catalogs Listed by Location.) The real advantage to this system is that you can read about a particular library online, then telnet directly to it from the Gopher.

In this lesson you learned where to find "directories" of information that will lead you to interesting and useful Internet resources. In the following appendix you'll find an Internet-command reference.

Appendix

UNIX Commands

Working With Files and Directories

Backspace	**Backspace, Ctrl+h, , #, Delete**
Clear the command line	**Ctrl+U or @**
Cancel an operation	**Ctrl+C or q**
Change directory	**cd /*directoryname***
Change directory: back one level	**cd ..** (make sure you leave a space after the **d**)
Change directory: back to your home directory	**cd**
Copy a file	**cp *oldname newname***
Copy a file to another *directoryname* directory	**cp *oldname***
Copy all files in directory and subdirectories to another directory	**cp -r * / *directoryname***
Copy several files to another directory	**cp *firstpartofname* * *directoryname***
Current directory: show path	**pwd**
Delete a file	**rm *filename***
List directory contents: full info and hidden files	**ls -al**
List directory contents: full information	**ls -l**

List directory contents: names only	**ls**
List directory contents: names only, several columns	**ls -x**
List directory contents: page by page	**ls	more** (**Spacebar** to continue, **q** to stop.)
List directory contents: full, page by page	**ls -l	more**
Log out	**Ctrl+d, logout, exit**
Move a file *directoryname*	**mv** *filename*
Password (change)	**passwd**
Read a text file	**cat** *filename*
Read a text file: page by page	**more** *filename*
Read the instruction manual	**man** *commandname* **??**
Rename a file *newname*	**mv** *originalname*
Repeat command	**!! or r**
Search for text in a file	**grep** "*this text*" *filename*
Search for text in all files, current directory	**grep** "*this text*" *
Search for text, don't show line	**grep -l** "*this text*" *
Search for text, don't worry about case	**grep -i** "*this text*" *
What's my login name?	**whoami** or **who am i**

Using FTP to Transfer Files

ASCII: prepare to transfer an ASCII file	**ascii**
Binary: prepare to transfer a binary file	**binary**

Change directory	**cd**
Change directory on *your* system	**lcd** (use like the cd command under "UNIX Commands," above)
Change directory to previous	**cdup** or **cd ..**
Close the connection	**close** or **disconnect**
Close the connection and exit FTP	**bye** or **quit** or **Ctrl+d**
Confirm transfer type	**type**
Connect to an FTP site	**open** *hostaddress* or **ftp** *hostaddress*
Current directory: show path	**pwd**
Directory listing: full	**dir**
Directory listing: names only	**ls**
Directory listing: names only, several columns	**ls -x**
Directory listing: include subdirectories and put in a text file	**ls -lR** *filename*
Exit FTP	**quit** or **bye** or press **Ctrl+d**
Extract files from a tar file	**tar xvf** *filename*
Hash marks indicate transfer progress	**hash**
Help: a list of FTP commands	**help** or **?**
Help: describe a command	**help** *commandname* or **?** *commandname*
Read a text file	**get** *filename* -
Read a text file using "more"	**get** *filename* - "	**more**" (**Spacebar** to continue, **Ctrl+c** to stop)

Search for text	**get** *filename* "	**grep** *word*"
Search for text, don't worry about the case	**get** *filename* "	**grep** -i *word*"
Transfer a file *from* the FTP site	**get** *sourcefile destinationname*
Transfer a file *to* the FTP site	**put** *sourcefile destinationname*
Transfer a file to your computer with Xmodem	**xmodem st** *filename* (text file) **xmodem sa** *filename* (Apple text file) **xmodem sb** *filename* (binary file)
Transfer a file *from* your computer with Xmodem	Replace the **s** in the previous commands with **r**.
Transfer a file to your computer with Zmodem	**sz** *filename filename etc.*
Transfer multiple files *from* the FTP site	**mget** *filename filename etc* or **mget** *partialname**
Transfer multiple files *to* the FTP site	**mput** *filename filename*
Uncompress UNIX compressed files	**uncompress** *filename*
View contents of a tar file	**tar tf** *filename*

Using Archie

Telnet to Archie

Search type, selecting	**set search** *type* (*type* may be **regex**, **exact**, **sub**, or **subcase**)

Search type, finding	**show search**
Searching	**prog** *filename*
Paging, turn on	**set pager**
Paging, turn off	**unset pager**
E-mail a list	**mail** *emailaddress*
E-mail, set e-mail address	**set mailto** *emailaddress*
Descriptive search	**whatis** *keyword*
View a list of FTP sites	**list**
View Archie help	**help**
View a list of Archie servers	**servers**
Maxhits, modify the number	**maxhits** *number*

Using Your Service Provider's Archie Client

Search	**archie -x** *filename* (replace *x* with **s** for sub, **e** for exact, **r** for regex, or **c** for subcase.)
Search, define host	**archie -x -h***hostname filename*
Search, define maxhits	**archie -x -m***number filename*
Search, simplified listing	**archie -x -l***filename*
Search, and save list in a file	**archie -x** *filename* *>savefilename*

Using UNIX Mail

Cancel a reply	**Ctrl+c Ctrl+c**
Delete messages	**d** *numbers*
Include a message in a Reply or Forward	**~f** *number*

Include a message in a Reply or Forward—use tab	~m *number*
Include a text file in the message	~r *filename*
Preserve a message (don't move from mailbox)	**pre**
Put a message in the text editor	**e** *number* **or v** *number*
Quit mail	**q**
Quit mail without removing messages	**x**
Read a message or several messages	*numbers*
Read message headers	**f** *numbers*
Read the current message, then reset current to next	**Enter**
Read the current message	**p**
Read the current messages header	**f**
Read the last message	**$**
Read the message before the current message	**- (hyphen)**
Read the top lines of messages	**top** *numbers*
Reply to a message, copy to all original recipients	**R** *number*
Reply to a message	**r** *number*
Save a message in a text file, remove the header	**w** *numbers filename*
Save messages in a text file	**s** *numbers filename*
Start a message	**mail** *address*

Starting mail	**mail**
Stop viewing message	**Ctrl+c or Ctrl+x**
Undelete messages	**u** *numbers*
View a list of messages	**h**
View the last pageful of messages	**z-**
View the next pageful of messages	**z**

Using WAIS (the Swais Version)

Deselect all selections	**=**
E-mail a document	**m**
Enter keywords on which to search	**w** and then press **Enter** (Press **Ctrl+c** to cancel)
Move the cursor down one entry	**j** or **down arrow** or **Ctrl+n**
Move the cursor down one screen	**J** or **Ctrl+v** or **Ctrl+d**
Move the cursor up one entry	**k** or **up arrow** or **Ctrl+p**
Move the cursor up one screen	**K** or **Ctrl+u**
Move to a particular line	type the **number** and press **Enter**
Quit	**q**
Read about the highlighted database	**v** or **,** (comma)
Reading a jumbled up document	Press **|** type **more**, and press **Enter**
Return to the listing	**s**

Search for a listing	Press / then type the **word** you are looking for, and press **Enter**
Search selected entries with keywords	**Enter**
Select an entry (or deselect a selected entry)	**Spacebar** or **.** (period)
Select an entry and move to keywords field	**Ctrl+j**
View the Help screen	**h** or **?**

Telnet Sessions

Connect to a Telnet site	**open** *hostaddress* or **telnet** *hostaddress*
Connect to an IBM mainframe	**tn3270** *hostaddress*
Closing a Telnet connection from the Telnet site	**quit**, **exit**, **Ctrl+d**, or **done**. Or try **Ctrl+]** followed by **close**.
Closing a Telnet connection from the telnet> prompt	**close**
Closing a Telnet session	**quit**, **q**, or **Ctrl+d**
Selecting an escape character	**set escape** *character*
Turning echo on and off	**set echo**
Suspend the session	**z**
Restart session	**fg** (in most cases)
View help	**?**

Using Gopher

Bookmarks: Add the current menu to the bookmark list	**A**
Bookmarks: Add the selected menu item to the bookmark list	**a**

Bookmarks: Delete a bookmark from the list	**d**
Bookmarks: View the list of bookmarks	**v**
Exit Gopher immediately (no confirmation)	**Q**
Exit the Gopher (the system will ask you to confirm)	**q**
Return to the main menu	**m**
Return to the previous menu	**u** or **left arrow**
Save a document or file	**s**
Search for a menu option	**/**
Transfer a document or file to your computer	**D**
View the next page in long menus	**Spacebar** or **>** or **+** or **PgDn**
View the previous page in long menus	**b** or **<** or **-** or **PgUp**

Using the World Wide Web (Line-Mode Browser)

Display the Help page	**h** or **help**
Display the WWW manual	**m** or **manual**
Go down one page	Press **Enter**
Go to a [*number*] reference	Type the ***number*** and press **Enter**.
Go to a document in the Recall list	**r** ***number*** or **recall** ***number***
Go to the first document you saw	**ho** or **home**
Go to the first page	**t** or **top**

Go to the last page	**bo** or **bottom**
Go to the previous document	**b** or **back**
Go to the previous page	**u** or **up**
List the documents you've seen	**r** or **recall**
Print a document	**print**
Quit	**quit**
Save in a file	**>** *filename*
Save in a file (append)	**>>** *filename*
Search a document for a keyword	**f** *keywords* or **find** *keywords* (only when you see FIND on the prompt line)
See a list of [ ] references	**l** or **list**
View the next reference from the last document	**n** or **next**

Index

C